ROD HUTCHINSON

CARP ALONG THE WAY

VOLUME TWO

INTO THE NINETIES...

PUBLISHED BY ANGLING PUBLICATIONS

First published in 2009

© Angling Publications Ltd. and Rod Hutchinson

British Library Cataloguing in Publication Data

Carp Along the Way - Volume Two
1. Carp Angling
1. Angling Publications Ltd

ISBN 978-1-871700-76-3

Compiled, designed and produced by Angling Publications Ltd.

Printed by MPG Books

OTHER BOOKS BY ROD HUTCHINSON

Rod Hutchinson's Carp Book
First published 1981. Reissued 2005.

The Carp Strikes Back
First published 1983. Second Edition 1984.
Reprinted 1986. Reissued 2006.

Carp Now And Then
Published 1988.

Rod Hutchinson's Guide To Carp Baits
Published 1989

Carp Along The Way, Volume One

ACKNOWLEDGEMENTS

Again special thanks to Kevin Clifford, Keith Hodson and
Dave Gawthorne for hunting down old articles from the past

Thanks to the various publications whose material is reproduced in
the pages that follow, including Angler's Mail, Coarse Fisherman,
David Hall's Coarse Fishing, Carpworld, Carp Fisher,
and my own Carpscene

Thanks to my old mates who feature in my recollections
of some of the more exciting and bizarre occurrences that have
littered my life and carp fishing experiences, including Mally Roberts,
Mad Tim 'The Big O' Richardson, Zyg Gregorek, Mark Lawson,
Keith 'The Tooth' O'Connor, Dave 'Big Un' Walker and wife Jane,
Johnny Allen, Albert 'Alf' Romp and Paul Woods, with apologies
to anyone I've missed out

Thanks to Big Dave and Mally for their flow of one-liners

Thanks also to those anglers whose photographic work I may have
inadvertently drawn on in the compilation of this book

Thanks also to Annie and the kids for our memorable
shared adventures

Again very special thanks to Tim Paisley for his ongoing
research into my material and pictures, and for pulling the
whole thing together

INTO THE NINETIES... **CONTENTS**

DEDICATION

This book is dedicated to Sue, Annie and Corrie, the three long-suffering women who have shared long periods of my life and have done their best to cope with my ongoing obsession with carp

And to daughters Kath and Emma and granddaughters Becky, Yasmin, Jessica, Amy and Lily

Foreword
by Tim Paisley

The first volume of Carp Along the Way ended with Rod speeding down to Savay in the early 80s in his 'Night Driving' piece. Because I travel long distances for almost all my carp fishing it is still one of my favourite of Rod's writings. The piece could have been from any era of Rod's carp fishing years with any of a thousand destinations in mind that he has had in his sights when he has left his Lincolnshire home at all hours of the day and night. For much of his life Rod's involvement with carp has gone beyond the addiction category to the all-consuming cloak of an obsession. For many, many years he simply had to carp fish, and he introduces this volume by reflecting on the fact that his obsession with carp has been damaging to some non-carp fishing aspects of his life, most particularly in terms of his 'permanent' personal relationships with the opposite sex.

As with the first volume the material in this book consists of a number of previous articles – some modified and extended – and a great deal of new, specially-written material. Obtaining new chapters from Rod is an unpredictable business! Working closely with him over a long period of time it becomes increasingly apparent just how inspirational his writing is. Starting with a framework of previously-published material which we thought was a suitable basis for the book I made the odd suggestion to Rod as to where there were gaps to be filled in. What I didn't realise when I made the suggestion was that when Hutchy sits down with a blank piece of paper in front of him he writes whatever looms largest in

Foreword

his head. What looms largest in his head invariably involves humorous memories of carp sessions and occasions, and carp people.

Roughly speaking Carp Along the Way, Volume Two covers the Eighties, through into the early Nineties. Dates don't really matter in the context of this book, other than provoking the need to explain one or two things. For instance Redmire happened in the early Seventies, but Rod's lovely 'Dream Come True' piece was written and published in Angler's Mail in the Eighties, and 'surfaced' after the first book was completed, so it appears here. The same can be said of the 'Wildies' chapter, which also dates back to the Seventies. The strange chapter 'Last Month's TV' was published in Coarse Fisherman in the Eighties and is included here because it is a priceless example of the bizarre workings of Rod's mind and pen, and merits a permanent record. Those of you who go back some time and are able to recognise the characters included in this chapter will understand that I come out of this rather well! (If you can accept that to be insulted by Rod is some sort of compliment!)

Conveniently the starting point is an interview Rod gave Coarse Fisherman's then-Editor Dave Phillips in 1985. It is convenient because it took place at about the time the first volume ended, and because it reminds all of us – and informs the uninformed – of Rod's beginnings and a few of his stunning successes from the Sixties through to the Eighties. Those of you who have read Volume One will be familiar with Rod's early carping career. Those of you who haven't read the first volume may be encouraged to obtain a copy!

There is no exact chronological sequence to the book, not even to the freshly-written material that appears in here! For instance as the compiler of the jigsaw of material I was a bit bemused to receive a new chapter supposedly relating to the Eighties which started, "Fast forward to April 2009"! But it is a memory of Johnny Allen, someone Rod was friendly with at Savay in the Eighties, which is why it falls within his memories of that period.

It isn't strictly true but in compiling these volumes it has been convenient to think of Rod's adult life in terms of the Sue years, the Annie years, and the Corrie years. The Sue years ended in the mid Eighties, and this was the marriage breakdown Rod reflects on in his Introduction and some of his time with Big Dave. The Annie years ended in the early Nineties, and the years spent with Annie and her children (from her previous marriage) are reflected in much of the material that appears herein. Corrie (Coral) is Rod's current partner and makes herself known to Rod in entertaining fashion in the final chapter of this book.

The previously-published material appeared in various publications, including Rod's annual Carpscene catalogue of the late Eighties and early Nineties, Coarse Fisherman, Carp Fisher, Carpworld, David Hall's Coarse Fishing Today and Angler's Mail. Thanks again to Kevin Clifford for his efforts in trolling through his extraordinarily comprehensive library of angling publications to unearth Rod's previously published work, in particular the stunning 'A Dream Come True' piece, which was new to me.

I've known Rod (if you ever get to 'know' Rod!) for 32 years and he never ceases to surprise me. Compiling one of his books is a labour of love, albeit a frustrating one at times. The completion of this one has been made doubly difficult by the fact that Rod has been suffering from increasingly troublesome cataracts, which have meant that his vision has been very impaired. (They've now been successfully operated on.) This has made writing difficult, re-reading previous material for amendments a non-starter, and identifying which pictures go with which chapter near-impossible! But to receive a new piece of material from this extraordinary writer is still an adventure. His Mally material – of which there will be a great deal more in Volume Three, no doubt – invariably has me in tears of laughter and joy, and his anecdotes of times spent with mates and friends are always a revelation. The frustration is that for all the words contained in the first two volumes Rod is still barely scratching the surface of what has happened during his carp fishing years, and life. He can talk for hours describing incidents I have no previous knowledge of and which have never been mentioned in print. I doubt he now has the self-discipline to write an actual autobiography but it would make a wonderful read if he could find it in himself to write such a work.

The material that appears here needs to be set in the context of Rod's two great Eighties' books 'The Carp Strikes Back' and 'Carp Now and Then'. Rod was at his most prolific fishing-wise and writing-wise during that decade and the material that appears in the pages that follow is simply a backdrop to the serious ('serious'? make that 'committed'!) and successful fishing Rod was involved in during that period. To read Rod's work without delving into his Savay, Colne Valley and Cassien adventures described in those books can lead to a very distorted and incomplete view of his successes and achievements.

When will Volume Three appear? Possibly next year, but certainly within the next two years. Rod's back-catalogue of writing over the last fifteen years or so has been surprisingly sparse. His recent carp-fishing activities have been limited because of Corrie's long term illness and Rod's own eyesight problems, and all carp writers need the inspiration of the actual fishing to keep the material flowing. We have some material for Volume Three but Rod's next book – which we are currently working on – will be a limited-edition 'Carp Inspirations', more of which anon.

Finally, please don't take everything Rod writes at face value. That is not to suggest that he is anything other than precise about his actual carp fishing, but when it comes to writing about friends he does indulge in the odd flight of fancy. Mally in particular appears to inspire these imaginative, though highly entertaining, journeys into the surreal. I raised this aspect with Rod, asking if they perhaps required some explanation, but he simply replied, "Keep the readers guessing!"

That's Rod all over. Since I first got involved with carp fishing almost forty years ago he has been a giant of a figure on the carp scene, and one who has always kept us guessing as to what will happen next in his life. I think and hope that 'Carp Inspirations' will happen next, but with Rod you can never be too sure of anything!

Tim Paisley, October 2009

Introduction

It was a full twenty years before I realised, in hindsight, just how obsessed I had become with carp in the Seventies and early Eighties. I thought I had a full rounded life with my family, music, still playing football and so on. Yet the reality was that my whole life now revolved around carp: studying them, fishing for them, and bait making as a living. Most of the trade I had was in the south – Essex, Kent, Surrey – basically anywhere around the M25 where gravel pits abounded as they were dug to feed the concrete appetites of our emerging motorway system. Every pit seemed to hold a few carp and big tench and I was keen to take advantage of this.

At the start of the Eighties my life ran in two-week cycles due to the week-on/week-off rota system of the Savay syndicate. Week one was my off week. The business was in its infancy and I was still working from home. I would spend three days in the garage, making bait and preparing orders. In the evening I would whip out for a couple of hours down at my local Castle Lake, which I knew like the back of my hand. There was a 'no night fishing' rule at Castle which suited me down to the ground. The best feeding times were seven till nine in the morning and the last hour in the evening. I could fit both of these in around my working day and by mid July, with the evenings starting to shorten, sneak a couple of pints in at my local pub on the way home. Depending on what orders I had I would leave home either early Wednesday morning, or early evening, to deliver orders to the dozen or so shops I had at that time that stocked my products. If I was away early I would stop at either Maxey or London Road Pits and fish the night before delivering to Sheltons at Peterborough. Then I'd move on to Penge Angling in Essex to make a start on the London deliveries before getting my head down on one of the pits that now skirt the M25. Finding a suitable lake was no problem: every shop I visited would put me onto a local lake that had a few carp in it.

In those far-off days the vast majority of lakes were uncrowded and very often, during the week, I had the lakes to myself. I didn't always catch because over the years I have found that in England most waters are more productive in daytime than at night, and most days I had to pack away my gear just as feeding was beginning. It had to be done: I had a hectic schedule. Although by then I was in my late thirties I was still playing football on a Saturday afternoon: consequently, besides the tackle which was in the van at all times, my football kit was, too! Very often I was so late back from south London that I would go straight to the game and not see Sue and the children till early Saturday evening. After all the years I had spent contract scaffolding around the country, when I was finally supposed to be living at home I was seeing even less of the family than when I was living away.

Still, every Saturday night was party night. A lot of the lads I had met at Savay and on my travels would come up religiously for the Saturday rave, then it was a case of up early – sometimes we didn't even go to bed – then off to Savay for our rota week. Not that we fished on a Sunday: it was a case of setting up the swim, get all washed up, decent clothes on, and a gang of us who were music freaks would be off to the Hammersmith Astoria – now the Apollo – where every Sunday all the top R & B, jazz and funk artists would play; artists like Luther Van Dross, Al Jarreau, Gwen Guthrie, George Benson, Ruby Turner, Al Green, Level 42 and so on. It was a great time. The elders of our gang, Roger Smith, Bob Jones, Johnny Allen, even Big Cliff Howard and I, would be back at the lake about half past midnight and start fishing. The younger guys would go on to a late-night disco club in Watford. Most were back around six in the morning, although those who pulled on a regular basis – no names mentioned! – we might not see for a couple of days!

I would generally pack up on the Wednesday morning before returning to the bait-making grind – although that was unless the fish were really on the feed. I hardly saw the family as things were but in 1983 I had my book The Carp Strikes Back published of which several thousand copies were sold to France, Belgium, Holland, Germany and, to a lesser extent the former Soviet bloc countries. I began to get invitations to fish in all these countries, many of which I accepted. The only problem was that where before my trips were three or four days they now became ten to fourteen days away.

I was caught up on a runaway carp train. When you find that you are naturally good at something you love doing it is very hard to stop doing it. If my life may have seemed chaotic to some it was actually worse than that! Returning home from a Lincolnshire lake in early springtime 1979 I spotted a couple of crane jibs about 500 yards off the main highway. I was intrigued and had to find out why they were there. I pulled off at the next junction and went back to see what was going on.

Down a long track that took some finding I came across two areas of about 15 acres apiece being dug out for their sand content. The top one of these pits, although still being dug, was already filled with water which was bright blue in the spring sunshine. It reminded me of the Blue Lake, Sundridge at Johnsons Lakes in Kent. All the lakes at Johnsons had produced very large carp and tench while they were still being worked.

I spoke to the crane drivers to find out who the owner was and what the plans were after extraction had been completed. It transpired that the top digging was to be left as a lake with the intention of putting a few trout in it. The bottom digging was to be reclaimed and filled up with the waste dug from the first lake. After all the travelling I had done in pursuit of big fish I just looked at the water and thought that here was the ideal environment to produce big fish, more or less on my doorstep. By the afternoon I had secured a long-term lease on the lake and entered into a labour of love which would last for the rest of my life. Woldview was born, and with it the new syndicate to fish the water.

I rarely seemed to have a spare moment. When I was tired I just jumped into the sleeping bag and slept, wherever I was. To compound things the fledglings had flown the nest. Emma was off, enjoying being a student at Teacher Training College, while Kath had just presented us with our first grandchild, the lovely Becky. Life had definitely changed. Kath's wedding had been the first time that I had witnessed a groom wearing twice as much make-up as the bride! But such is life...

Sometimes you don't realise the casualties you leave behind. It is little wonder that after twenty three years of putting up with me my wife had had enough. I was as gutted as a kipper. I'd never seen it coming, but it was time to get my coat on and leave.

But life goes on and after a few months of craziness and haziness I was still there, in body at least. Meanwhile my brain was being studied at the local polytechnic! I came through it all, and the path was clear. I had to get the carp obsession out of my head and the only way to do that was to fish and fish until I'd had enough of it and it was out of my system. The world was my oyster. I was a single man again, free to go anywhere I fancied in the world. I'd come through the coma of self-pity and life was looking good when, what happens? That old devil called love struck again. I didn't want it: I certainly didn't need it; but I was consumed by it. I tried to fight it; tried to explain that I had to travel, to be away; that fishing was the basis of my living, and that I didn't have an ordinary nine till five job.

"No problem," said Annie, my new lady, "we'll come with you. The kids will enjoy it. It will be an adventure."

And that it was. An adventure it certainly was. As an experience I still haven't worked it out. It all happened so fast I could hardly keep

Rod the author enjoying a book and magazine signing session.

pace with it. For the next few years my carp fishing would be very different from my past. Venues would have to suit the family. There would have to be provisions to feed them and, as everyone knows, children are hungry all the time. There would be no more getting by for a week on a box of Weetabix, a packet of biscuits and cadging cups of tea off anyone I could find. Even 'guesting' with the camper van and a family looked highly unlikely, but then you never could tell.

If life had never been the same before, it would certainly never be the same again. The years that followed from the mid Eighties through to the early Nineties – was it really such a short period of time? – are still something of a blur. Perhaps reliving them through some of the pages that follow will help make more sense of it all, although somehow I doubt it!

1985 Interview

"I can see myself carp fishing for the rest of my days.
I've never set myself any targets. The fish I've caught
have just come along. You catch big fish by fishing
waters with big fish in them. My favourite carp is the
next one I hook."

Rod is larger then life in every respect. He exceeds six feet in height with inches to spare and is one of life's natural extroverts. Every specimen hunter, including those who have never met him, can relate outrageous Hutchinson tales. Some have no foundation; most are wildly exaggerated. All seem to revolve around his drinking prowess, his passion for Indian food, his repertoire of gags and, of course, his magical ability in wasting no time in pulling big carp out of the most difficult waters. Rod was born into a fishing family, but not in the angling sense. His relations worked in the trawling industry of his native Grimsby, an industry which flourished back in 1945 when Rod arrived on the scene. Yet although angling played little or no part in the lives of Rod's immediate family he was bitten by the angling bug at the tender age of five when his maternal grandmother took him down to the local docks. Over to Rod...

We all had to start somewhere! One of my earliest carp.

Tench were my main quarry for a number of years, as this huge bag shows.

"I saw some guys catching sea trout and decided that I wanted some of that! I got my first taste of coarse fishing a couple of years later when the docks were stocked with coarse fish. But it was the festivities of the Coronation celebrations in 1953 that really got me interested in bigger fish. Activities organised for the Grimsby youngsters included the usual gamut of street parties and, more importantly, a trip out to the countryside. The older guys intended fishing, so I decided to take my tackle along. In those days my rod consisted of an old billiard cue with staples hammered into it!" laughed Rod.

At the pits that day young Rod watched in fascination as an older angler caught some tench. Having already taken a liking to the open countryside and the crystal clear waters of the gravel pits Rod decided to get himself some tench action.

"Within a very short period of time I too was catching tench," said Rod. "I used to catch a bus out into the countryside and fish for tench. The fish in the pits were a lot bigger than those I used to catch in the docks. But really it was a little later, when I was about twelve, that I got

1985 Interview

bitten by the specimen hunting spirit. I read an article by Fred J. Taylor all about catching pike on herrings. I knew of a lake which held some pike and although I had never caught any I went along and cast out a herring. Soon afterwards I was away and landed a 12½lb pike, which happened to break the lake record! I beat that a week later when I landed a fifteen-pounder!

In the age we were brought up in me and my mates were lucky when it came to specimen hunting. We had a canal with a good head of roach over 2lb, and up to 3lb: there were a number of pits with perch over 3lb, and Castle Lake was a tremendous tench water. By the time I was fourteen years old I considered myself an experienced specimen hunter."

During his early specimen hunting years Rod had accidentally caught a carp while fishing for tench, but he admits that to start with it didn't set off the carp bug.

"At that time a carp was considered a once-in-a-lifetime experience," he explained. "Then in 1960 a club which had taken control of one of the small pits stocked it with carp. I caught ten the first day they went in! They were only small – up to 6lb or so – and I've still got photos of some of them. Once I realised that carp could be caught I started travelling round Lincolnshire trying to catch bigger ones.

It was during that stage that I found a small pond that had been overstocked with very small carp. I decided that they were stunted and moved some of them on to other waters. I didn't know any better at that stage, and in any case at that time in the sixties moving carp wasn't frowned on the way it is now. But I'm not too ashamed of what I did for those little carp I moved all those years ago are now the forebears of most of the big carp in Lincolnshire. I think I can claim to have given enjoyment to thousands of carp anglers!"

Amongst the consignments of carp moved on by Rod were some small fish placed into Castle Lake. These grew very quickly in their new rich environment and by the late sixties Rod was catching good numbers of double-figure carp.

"Good doubles those days were the equivalent of good twenties these days (1985). They were still very rare. About 1967 or '68 I can remember writing to Jim Gibbinson and telling him I had been catching a few carp. I said I'd had fourteen doubles that year but had lost about as many again, and asked him what I was doing wrong. He replied that if he had landed fourteen doubles that year he would have been over the moon!"

Rod's angling horizons broadened in 1964 when he married his first wife Sue. She was from Bromley in Kent and it was during trips down to see his new in-laws that Rod started fishing the carp waters of Kent.

"Some of the anglers I met in Kent included up-and-coming

My first wife was from Kent so I was fishing southern waters as long ago as the Sixties. This brace of doubles is from Horton Kirby.

A multiple carp catch from a local Lincolnshire water.

specimen kids, people who went on to become well-known anglers. I did well in Kent. The fishing was easier because there were more carp and more carp waters. I learned a lot because at that time the specials were just taking off. They were popularised by Gerry Savage and Jim Gibbinson, but everyone was using them. I went back to Lincolnshire and applied the same baits and methods to my local waters. Ironically it was around this time – probably in '68 or '69 – that I developed what has become looked on as my particle-bait theory. Special baits didn't seem to work on one particularly hard water known as Pinetrees Pool. I started to use hemp on there. At that time there had been a ban on hemp on Throop because the barbel were supposed to get preoccupied on it. It seemed to me that the carp might get preoccupied on hemp, too, because I believed that in their natural feeding they became preoccupied on bloodworm. It just seemed a logical idea. At the time I thought the method would only work on certain types of waters; waters which were silty and where the carp lived mainly on bloodworms and the like. On most of the other waters I fished at the time I thought the specials were the best approach, although I have learnt since that there are no hard and fast rules in carp fishing. With baits and methods it's a case of waters and fish being horses for courses.

I think it's out there, and it's all been written now. Both types of baits are available and anyone who doesn't take advantage of the situation is a fool. Specials, boilies and particles can all be winners on their day."

In 1972 Rod gained a place on the Redmire syndicate. I asked him how he had managed to get into the most exclusive carp water of all.

"I had been a BCSG member since the group was formed and

Early doubles from the A1 Pits.

Pinetrees Pool success in the Seventies. This hard little water taught me more about carp's behaviour than any other water I had fished up to that time.

of course I had been to Kent and done a bit. When you fished Kent regularly and caught a few fish you got talked about and met the right people. Also I'd written a few articles by then as well. I wasn't overawed by Redmire. I'm not a romantic. It wasn't the mystique or anything like that, although I did feel a sense of history when I first fished there. It never looked the most beautiful of waters when I fished there, and it still doesn't! At the time I thought I was fishing for record breakers.

I did see a very big common in Redmire, but just how big it was I wouldn't like to say. In my judgement commons never weigh as heavy as mirrors of the same length. But that fish was certainly far longer than the carp that was eventually to become Chris Yates's record. I was very successful at Redmire, catching numerous big fish to 32½lb, but somehow I fell victim to the then all-too-familiar Redmire aggro. I wasn't aware of it at the time but other syndicate members later rang me to tell me I had been upsetting some of the others.

As far as I was concerned Redmire was a carp lake. When the Redmire fish weren't feeding I would go to the pub just the same as

I would on any other carp water. But some members thought I was disrespectful to the water, which they regarded as some sort of holy shrine. When I caught more fish than them it rubbed salt into their wounds. Yet nobody loved Redmire more than Chris Yates, and he would come with me to the pub! There was nothing nicer than getting back onto the bank just as the sun was going down and finishing off a bottle of brandy."

After three seasons on Redmire it all came to an end. It is widely believed that Rod was the first syndicate member to be expelled from the water, but Rod insists that he was the first well-known member to get the push.

"It appears that one of the members had been rude to a farm hand

On my travels again, this time to Waveney Valley's G Lake, where particles scored heavily for me.

I spent three years in the Redmire syndicate and had some tremendous results there. These three big twenties fell to my hemp and seed approach.

– had threatened to kill him or something. At that time it was thought a good enough excuse to get rid of me! Apparently someone had been rude, but it turned out it was someone off another rota; someone with short dark hair, and who drove a different car to mine. I felt bitter at the time, but I soon got over it. Life goes on.

When I left Redmire I thought the usual thoughts. Where can you go after Redmire? But in the three years I had been a member a lot of things had happened to carp fishing, and a lot of waters had started to overtake Redmire as big carp waters. When you are in Redmire you are so engrossed with the pool that you don't realise what is going on in the outside world.

The first carp water I fished after Redmire was Cuttle Mill. It was a culture shock, but then the old indicators started flying up and down and first chuck in resulted in a twenty pounder. It was good fun!"

Among the waters Rod has fished since those Redmire days is Savay Lake, the Buckinghamshire gravel pit where he has enjoyed tremendous success with big carp. Rod was – and still is – a member of the famous Looney rota, a group of accomplished and successful carp men who have caught a lot of carp, and thoroughly enjoyed themselves at the same time.

"There are a lot of quotes flying around from those days. One of the members is supposed to have said: 'I've sussed out why Hutchinson is so successful – he brings everyone else down to his level.' It was really a reaction to all the seriousness in carp fishing. A number of good anglers finally became aware that you don't have to live, breathe and eat carp fishing: you can enjoy yourself and still catch big carp. At first I was the only angler with that attitude, but those who joined in became more relaxed and caught more than they had ever done before. It was the spirit of the time: we really did have a fabulous time. 1982 and 1983 were the most enjoyable years I've ever had. Six thirties in a season can't be bad!"

These days of course Rod is involved in angling on a professional basis as proprietor of Catchum Products, supplying bait and tackle to specialist anglers. Why did he decide to go into business?

"I never wanted to; it was a case of necessity! I was getting too old for what I was doing, scaffolding and steeplejack work. It suited me at the time. I could work for short periods and earn a lot of money, but as the country went down the nick and the recession arrived a lot more people came into the game. The money you could earn was cut to a pittance and it wasn't worth the risk any more. The industry had become flooded with cheap labour. I had to do something. At 36 you've got to put your mind to something! I had been preparing bait for a few friends for a number of years, but I didn't really want to get involved in that. I thought I might earn a living from selling rods and

After I left Redmire I wandered around, with Cuttle Mill being one of my target waters. This is one of the twenties I had from the famous Midlands venue.

Savay was my main target during the early Eighties.
This is just one of my big fish from the famous southern gravel pit.

specialist tackle and writing the odd book, but the demand was for bait: everyone wanted bait! It seemed that no one knew how to make a decent carp bait."

Despite his business status Rod has strong views on the way that commercialisation is creeping into specialist angling as it becomes obvious that catching big fish can be worth money.

"I don't write articles which read like tackle and bait catalogues. I dislike the blatant commercialisation that I read in articles and news reports these days. I would like to see some sort of distinction drawn between what are adverts and what are articles. People should realise by now that carp – and any other big fish – aren't difficult to catch. When they are feeding you should catch them, and thousands of anglers are now discovering this."

Rod admits he is an angler purely for his own enjoyment and catches carp on his own terms. He fishes for carp because they are the fish that give him the most enjoyment.

A big fish from Cassien, the big-fish French venue that first hit the headlines in the early Eighties.

"An average carp is a good fish to catch and it pulls your string a bit. I've never gone on a non-stop 24-hour fishing session in my life. I refuse to even wet a line unless I am certain there are carp in the swim, and they are feeding. I don't want to waste any time fishing during unproductive periods," he insists.

Rod is often described as a 'natural angler', but he dismisses this suggestion. He reckons it is all down to watercraft, which in turn is the accumulation of many years of experience on the bank. Rod put this watercraft to good effect a couple of months back when he fished Lake Cassien in the south of France.

"A carp is a carp, wherever you catch it. I travelled over 1,000 miles to Cassien to fish a 2,500 acre water I didn't know and I did the business. In fact those big carp meant more to me because if I had beaten my previous best of 39¼lb in this country it would have been with a fish I had caught before, or I knew about. I went out to Cassien hoping to catch, while there are waters in this country where I would expect to catch. It was a great big challenge. I knew that a lot of anglers had been out there before us and completely blanked: relatively few had caught. I like the lifestyle of fishing abroad. For years while my family went abroad for their holiday I went fishing in this country instead, but once I went out there I got to love the sun and sangria. The highlight of my year is now going abroad."

I asked Rod how he reacted to the tales of some English specimen hunters who complained about the antics of the Cassien tourists, bathers and windsurfers...

"You must be joking! Anybody who complains about beautiful young girls with no clothes on has got to be taking his fishing too seriously. It makes for beautiful scenery, and it certainly doesn't put the fish off!"

What of the future?

"I can see myself carp fishing for the rest of my days. I've never set myself any targets. The fish I've caught have just come along. You catch big fish by fishing waters with big fish in them. My favourite carp is the next one I hook."

A Dream Come True

I should explain that because of the three-rota system at Redmire Pool fishing the opening there was, at best, a once-in-three-years experience. As it turned out I was only in the syndicate for three years, so fishing the off at Redmire for me turned out to be a once-in-a-lifetime experience! I will always treasure the memories of that opening.

Though nowadays an angler can fish for carp all the year round if he so wishes, be it laid out in the sun beside some French or Spanish lake, or putting up with the drizzle down in the West Country, there is still nothing to match the magic of the true 'off' when the clock strikes midnight heralding the start of the new English season. It is a moment you have anticipated for weeks, maybe months. Will your well-laid plans bring the success you have hoped for? Will your new rod be up to the job? Will that rig you have dreamt up really make all the difference? Is that bait you have been recommended really that good?

There are so many maybes, so many doubts, so many hopes, and only the coming of the new season can provide the answers. If indeed you have got it wrong somewhere along the line at least you can do something about inadequate tackle, incorrect choice of bait or rig, but it takes two to tango. Mother Nature must play her role. If she's in one of her moods and presents you with a lake that looks like a lawn for the start there is very little you can do about it. To get the full satisfaction out of the pursuit of carp whether or not you catch you have to enjoy being there. Having said that while you are enjoying being by the lake you may as well do your very best to ensure you catch a fish or two. I know from what I've seen and heard there are a great many anglers who simply go through the motions. There is a great deal more to carp fishing than simply banging out a bed of boilies, casting your bait into it, sitting back and leaving the rest up to the fish. You have to have alternative tactics in mind should your number one plan not work out on the day.

This is all the more relevant at the start of the season, for there are a great many waters in which the carp appear to change their habits year by year. What has been the going bait or method the previous season can often flop entirely the following year, so go prepared for any circumstances. Boilies, floaters, particles, even a few naturals, you should have all these with you so there is no excuse if the fish are on the top or feeding on natural food. I feel a large part of being successful

What better place to start the season than Redmire Pool?
It was a once-in-a-lifetime experience. Sunrise over Greenbanks.

is down to confidence. If you know you have the bait and tackle to cope with every eventuality then you are confident from the start. Tell yourself that you are going to catch and that it's just a question of sorting out the best method.

Every 16th June is special but I suppose the one I was most excited about was in June 1973. I was a privileged man in that I was going to fish Redmire for the start of the season. At that time the legendary pool was the most magical water in the Universe. It was in the days before the rigs and boilies methods, a time when the capture of any carp was considered a feat. Indeed it was a time when Redmire definitely held fish far in excess of Dick Walker's then-record carp.

The thought of fishing that week had been with me every minute of the winter months. It wasn't a question of thinking which bait, but which baits. Just in case the weed was already on the top a variety of floaters would be needed. Then there was the choice of a long-term bait, not too visual as to scare fish out of an area after they had been caught on it. This would be a bait which was found through natural feeding, rather than one which attracted fish into an area. My choice here was mini maple peas, about half the size of a standard pea and dark brown, rather like a large tare. It probably shows the level of confidence that I had at the time as I had never used mini maples before or heard of anyone else doing so, but everything about them said they were right for the job.

Also I wanted a large flat bait which would rest easily on the silt, and a visual bait which would pick off sight feeders. I didn't expect such a bait to work for long, but during the first few weeks of the season there are always a few less cautious fish around likely to fall for this type of visual presentation. Here I chose broad beans, again a bait I hadn't used before, or heard of anyone else using but again it felt right. In addition to these baits I had taken with me a few buckets of mini worms, a few tins of Bacon Grill, assorted dry flies and 10lb of hemp.

Three days before the off my clapped-out old Morris Traveller rattled over the cattle grid at the entrance to the estate. Down in the

I arrived three days early and fired bait into every
likely feeding area. The famous pool at sunset.

valley the pool was tranquil and clear. We were in luck, the dreaded weed had yet to flourish. Everywhere I looked there were carp feeding hard, betraying their presence by the huge clouds of bubbles they threw up and the water stained red by suspended particles of clay disturbed by the rooting fish. I had the lake to myself and three full days to decide on my choice of swim before the off, so there was no rush to get my tackle out. I did, however, want to get the new baits introduced so I was straight round the lake firing both the peas and broad beans into every likely feeding area.

Once the bait introduction had been completed I made my way to the highest tree where I perched for the rest of the day just watching the movements of the fish and trying to get into the rhythm of the lake. This is often referred to as 'reading a water' and is a bit difficult to explain. What it amounts to is that if you observe the behaviour of the carp in a given water you will eventually see that in certain conditions the fish will favour certain areas. When the prevailing conditions change other areas will be preferred. It is more than just the changing of the wind, although that obviously plays a part. It is also about watching the reactions of the fish, if any, to fly hatches and bands of daphnia. For instance cloudy days and dawn and dusk are all good feeding periods with a low light intensity. Would it not, therefore, be likely that below a thick band of daphnia the same low light conditions would prevail and encourage feeding?

By evening the excitement was really mounting within me as huge golden scaled backs started rolling over the baited areas. Around mid-morning of day two I was perched amongst the branches of a tree overlooking Ingham's swim. Beneath the tree I had introduced a carpet of mini maples hoping the odd fish would move in and I could observe the manner in which they fed on the baits. I'd been there half an hour when light cloud started masking the sun. It was as if someone had shouted "Dinner-time" for suddenly fish started rolling all round the pool. Looking down at my bed of mini maples I couldn't believe my eyes. Five carp were feeding hard on them, and these were no ordinary carp. One was instantly recognised as Tom Mintram's 38lb mirror, the story of the capture of which is told in Jack Hilton's book 'Quest for Carp'. The fish had been caught the previous season by both John MacLeod and Jack Hilton, both times turning the needle on the scales to over 40lb. Here was a perfect yardstick to gauge the weight of the other fish by and the miraculous thing was that three of the other fish were bigger!

All were commons; one I estimated to be two inches longer than the big mirror, one was three inches longer and one at least five inches longer! What such fish would weigh would be pure speculation. In my experience common carp do not normally weigh as much per length as mirrors, many taking on a lean, almost wild appearance with age. However there was no doubt in my mind that beneath me I had at least one carp of record proportions feeding hard on my baits. To say I wasn't tempted to get a rod out would be untrue, but somehow the temptation was resisted.

Within fifteen minutes the giant fish had cleared the pound or so of maples beneath the tree and drifted off to my left before once more turning on a small mound about ten feet out from the bank midway between my position and the Stile Swim. This was another good sign as again it was an area I had baited. My choice of swim had been made for me. The Stile it had to be.

Twice more that day I baited the general area of the swim with approximately three pounds of maples. Within minutes of each baiting fish appeared and started feeding. I couldn't wait for the off. I was willing the time away, praying the conditions would not change. It all seemed so unreal.

Watching the pool it was obvious that one particular fish came out several times in the margin of the opposite bank close to a fallen elm known as Bowskill's tree. Creeping round I sat on the bank and watched until the fish rolled again so I could fix its precise position. Once this had been ascertained I scattered about eight ounces of broad beans around the area.

The dream becomes reality. An opening night catch of a 20lb+ leather
for me and a lovely 25lb mirror for Yatesy.

Some time in the early hours I drifted off to the land of never-
ending runs, only waking on the arrival of my fellow carp hunter Chris
Yates. I told him of the big fish, about their feeding hard on the baits,
and everything else that had gone on. The excitement was so great you
could reach out and grab it. The conditions were holding up and the
carp were still feeding. There was no way we could blow this one. If we
didn't catch this time we had no right to call ourselves carp anglers.

Early in the evening the third member of our rota, Bob Jones, then
holder of the eel record, arrived.

"How many have you had then?" asked Bob, knowing I had been at

Syndicate leader Jack Hilton arrived and set up in Ingham's Swim. Jack's pictured here with his first carp from the water in 1968, the famous Pinky at 35lb. It was through Jack that I got to fish the pool.

the lake for three days. When I told him I'd not even set up my rods he went on to tell me of past fish which had been caught before the off. I found this rather sad. To me it devalues the capture. I'd had a chance of what I considered to be a record fish but what would it have meant if I'd cheated? Midnight on the 15th June was what we planned for. To start earlier would dilute the magic of that moment.

By eight we all had our swims prepared and I had once more rebaited heavily with the mini maple peas. Chris was going to start with sweetcorn and broad beans on alternate rods; Bob, I believe, sweetcorn and kidney beans. We were all set up and there were still four hours to go so it was decided a couple of pints to toast the new season were in order.

We were back by ten, in time for any last minute alterations to our tackle or our swims. After watching the fish constantly for three days I had come to the conclusion the carp were now coming to the sound of the peas hitting the water; good numbers of fish, too, who made short work of the food I put in. Once it had gone the fish would be gone, too, so I decided to bait up once more in the minutes prior to midnight hoping, indeed expecting, this to draw the fish into the swim.

All settled in with baits already on the hooks dangling from the rod tips we were filled with an air of expectancy. I had told Chris previously of my plans to bait up when he called across "Fifteen minutes to go," and this was the signal for my baiting barrage. For ten solid minutes out went the thousands of peas I had pinned all my faith in. The night was warm and muggy, the sweat on my forehead attracting a halo of midges. There followed a few minutes of eerie silence until in the distance a church clock chimed and Chris called across, "Midnight".

Out sailed my bait to the small mound to the right of the swim. Here the depth was no more than three feet yet the line continued snaking from the spool. For a moment I thought I had missed the mound and it had dropped into deeper water. Then the penny dropped! Nowhere in the whole lake was there sufficient depth for that to happen. I put in the pickup and bent the rod hard over my shoulder. A carp was on, one that had taken my bait on the drop!

The fight was short but furious, most of it taking place in the margin beneath the rod top. I slipped the net into the water; a big heave on the rod, up came the fish then down she went into the folds of the net.

"Yippee!" I screamed at the top of my voice. Into my weigh bag and onto the scales: a Redmire leather of 22¼lb of pure magic. The dreams, the anticipation, the expectations had been great but the reality was even better! The time? Three minutes past midnight!

The magic of the night continued: it was the kind of opening all anglers dream of. All three of us hooked fish, Bob being unfortunate when his hook pulled free, ending his fight with an unseen monster. I was well pleased to tackle one of the immaculate Redmire commons, even though it fell short of the magical 20lb barrier, while Chris eventually won a hard-fought battle with a gorgeous mirror of 25lb.

With the coming of dawn we showed off our prizes for Bob's waiting camera. It had been such a start, such a happy occasion that I swear even the fish smiled! It was what those long months of waiting had been all about.

Bob had to leave around midday, his rigid schoolteacher schedule not taking into account such things as the start of the fishing season. Soon after Bob left Jack Hilton, the boss of the syndicate arrived, his gleaming Jaguar looking as though it had somehow got lost and arrived at the wrong function so out of place did it look parked next to Chris's beat-up Renault van and my ancient Moggy Traveller.

Meanwhile Chris and I enjoyed the afternoon on the shallows...

A Dream Come True

It was a magnificent leather, this time weighing 24lb.

After hearing of the fish I'd seen Jack elected to fish Ingham's Swim. Meanwhile Chris and I enjoyed the afternoon on the shallows, taking a succession of small carp up to 11lb on either free-lined or float-fished sweetcorn. Behind the tiny Wasp Island the water was black with fish but because of the bankside foliage casting to them was all but impossible, so we waded out in our underpants. Perched against the island as still as herons we became part of the landscape as fish swam around our feet. Most were small, all being commons, like peas in a pod. Occasionally the odd double-figure fish would drift in, to which we would present a bait. One of these took my offering on sight and the moment I set the hook it went crazy, shooting straight through my legs, then running twice around Chris, tying him up in the process! We burst into laughter, but we knew we were so privileged: had anyone experienced such events before? It was better than walking on the moon.

By early evening there was not a cloud in the sky and the sun was having a profound effect on the weed, which I swear was growing before our eyes. The moon came up big and bright. Even at midnight I could clearly make out Chris on the opposite bank, so light was the night.

The conditions had changed and now the pool seemed devoid of fish. I crawled into the sleeping bag not expecting any action but sometime around two I was woken by a fish crashing out. Looking up a bank of cloud had masked the moon and that was all it had taken to get a few fish feeding. Crash! Out in the pool there it was again. No doubt about it the fish were rolling off the submerged tree on the opposite bank. I whistled to Chris as the fish wasn't far from his position but there was no answer. He was obviously asleep.

Crash! Out it came again: a gift horse if ever I had seen one. Taking just one rod, landing net, a couple of rests and a pocket full of broad beans I crept round the pool to the spot on the bank adjacent to where the fish had shown. It was in exactly the same position as I'd seen it two nights earlier. I watched for a few moments just to make sure which end its head was before lowering a free-lined broad bean in front of it. Putting the rod on the rests I fixed a tube of silver foil between reel and butt ring for bite indication before lying back on the damp dew covered grass.

I rolled a cigarette and concentrated on the silver foil. The fish rolled again and in doing so must have caught the line because the foil indicator jumped up six inches or so before falling back. I nearly had a heart attack! The old ticker was pounding away so hard I felt certain the fish would hear it and be scared off. I was shaking so hard with nervous tension the cigarette in my hand looked like a sparkler! Eyes back on the water I saw the fish turn and head out into open water, its back clearly visible above the surface. As it did so the silver paper glided up to the butt ring.

Putting my hand over the spool I gingerly bent the rod into the fish. With no more than 12ft of line between the fish and the rod top it was no occasion for a heavy strike, even so my almost gentle strike caused some real fireworks to explode, the fish going crackers in the shallow margin before eventually beaching itself. I scooped it up in the big net and whispered to it, "I told you I'd have you sonny Jim." It was another magnificent leather, this time weighing 24lb. I cradled her like a baby before sacking her up off the dam wall for the night.

By dawn the sky had cleared again and with it the carp had disappeared. Meanwhile the weed continued to grow before our eyes. In the clear conditions even our afternoon excursions up onto the shallows tiddler-bashing became hard work. For three days and nights nothing at all moved and the pool had an unnatural stillness about it. As I snuggled into the sleeping bag on the third night I made a silent prayer: "Dear God give me a cloudy sky and a warm breeze and I promise to be a good boy."

Mid afternoon the following day my prayer was answered. I was at the top of a tree when up sprang the gentlest of breezes heading into the corner of the dam. Seemingly out of nowhere carp materialised following the breeze as if it were the Pied Piper. I couldn't get to my tackle quickly enough and within minutes had managed to crawl

It was one of the pool's most prized occupants, a 20lb+ common.

beneath an overhanging tree just to the right of the dam corner. The
area was one mass of weed with just the occasional small hole in it. Into
one of these I lowered the hookbait followed by a handful of peas. I'd
been sitting there maybe ten minutes when Tom Mintram – who had
arrived the previous day and was fishing just up from me in the Evening
Swim – crept up to see if I fancied a cup of tea. Such an offer couldn't
be refused.

Sitting out of sight on the other side of the tree with Tom I was
just putting the cup to my lips when my buzzer burst into life. Before
I could get to the rod the fish had bolted through about 20 yards of
weed and was solid. There was nothing I could do but go in after it,
winding down all the time as I did so. Chris acted as ghillie, picked up

the net and followed me into the lake.

Luckily for me the fish hadn't made the deep water and I was able to get over the mass of weed he was enclosed in. Bending the rod for all I was worth the fish and weedbed rose slowly to the surface whereupon Chris netted the lot. It was so heavy it took the two of us to lift the mass of weed onto the bank.

We took so long to clear the weed away I was starting to doubt whether or not we'd actually got the fish but eventually there it lay in the bottom of the net, its pride bruised but its appearance immaculate. It was one of the pool's most prized occupants, a 20lb plus common.

The gods and the improved weather conditions stayed with us for the rest of the week and the carp continued to feed. Many more fish were to fall to our rods, mainly double-figure commons to me, while Chris added two more twenties to his impressive list, the second of which fell to tiddler-snatching in the shallows!

But all good things come to an end, and eventually that very special opening week drew to a close and we reluctantly left the carp-filled oasis that is Redmire Pool and made our way back to the real world.

We'd had a lot of fun and caught some magnificent fish. It was an opening week all carp anglers dream of. Keep the dream alive and one day it will happen for you!

Wildies

For many years I regarded the hard-fighting reputation of wild carp as pure myth. Anglers who caught them and gave them this reputation only did so – or so I thought – as an excuse for not catching large king-carp strains. The fight of wildies was said to be harder, faster, and in every respect better than a king carp. There was no way I could go along with this. I had caught heaps of wildies, yet not one had taken more than a couple of minutes to subdue. True, the rate of knots at which the indicators belted out was enough to get anyone's adrenalin flowing, but once the hook hit home what followed was very much an anti-climax.

Wildies are built for speed. They are long, almost chub-like, and they have just not got the flank on them for an enduring battle. They would make one long run on picking up the bait, but as soon as the rod was bent in they came splashing to the surface. A couple of mouthfuls of air and they'd had it. You could wind them in.

True, the average size of wildie I had caught had been very small, five pounds being a decent fish, but that did not alter my disrespect for them. That was until I fished a certain small, well-reeded lake for the first time. My intention had been to fish for tench, but a remarkable chorus of clooping soon saw me getting the carp rods out. That night I was fortunate enough to land an 11¼lb wildie, which took all of half an hour to land. If it had been daytime and I'd been familiar with the lake I would probably have landed the fish in half that time. Even if I had done so it would still have been one hell of a long battle.

There is much speculation as to whether or not the big wildies we fish for now are true wild-bred fish, or have a few king carp genes in them. To me it is irrelevant whether or not old granny had some fat old mirror sniffing round her in her hey day. As far as I am concerned if it looks like a wildie, fights like a wildie, then it is a wildie!

To make sure that the fight from that first fish wasn't a one-off I visited the lake many more times. Eventually I succeeded in taking another fish of 10¾lb. The fight was identical; fast, powerful and prolonged. I would like to have fished that lake more often but the matchmen on the committee decided to ban night fishing. Why I just don't know, as none of them fished nights anyway, but they obviously reckoned that if they were not gong to night fish then neither was anyone else!

On losing this opportunity wildies were cast from my mind. Local lakes holding double-figure fish being few and far between I broadened my horizons, taking in the large gravel pit complexes of the southern counties. Many of these pits had lain fallow for years, the only stocking they had received being when other pits in the area had either dried up or been back-filled, situations in which the fish would often be rescued and dropped into the non-fished pits.

Fishing Johnsons lake in Kent which surprised me by producing a brace of hard-fighting wildies.

It was on such a water that Brian and I found ourselves during the hot July of '76. We hadn't planned to fish any particular lake but just dropped in on any that took our fancy. The fishing turned out to be good with a couple of nice carp taken in the first two days. During our third night I hit a fish which I just could not control. It was the first time this had happened to me, getting stuck into an unstoppable fish. On feeling the hook it had just run out in a direct line away from me and

They were like peas in a pod. A brace of bionic wildies from Johnsons.

nothing I could do would make it deviate from its course. It carried on through a thick mass of submerged bushes, and then all went solid. Game over!

Such an event obviously created a great deal of discussion between Brian and me. What the hell was it? A big carp? Well I'd never hooked one like that before. A pike? No chance! They are supposed to scrap a bit in Loch Lomond, but elsewhere the fight isn't worth talking about.

Maybe the water held cats? Now that was something worth thinking about.

At 8.00 a.m. I had a run which was so fast that the rod was bouncing in the rests. On feeling the hook the fish went in a straight line for the submerged bushes, just as the unknown fish had done, but this time I was lucky and managed to keep it from the bushes. I had to point the rod at the fish to gain any control because mere rod pressure had the rod in a semi-circle and the corks creaking on the butt!

After about ten minutes I had the fish close enough to contemplate netting it, although we had not at this point seen what this veritable torpedo of a fish was. Brian dipped the net and I gave a veritable heave of the fish in that direction. What happened next no words can describe. On seeing the net the fish literally shot off like one of those rocket-fuelled drag racing cars. One second it was in front of us; the next it was swirling on the surface fifty yards away. Our reaction to this still puzzles me today: we both fell over laughing! It was the shock I suppose.

By this time I was thinking in terms of a 30lb plus something or other. Ten hard-fighting minutes later it lay in the landing net. We just could not believe what we were looking at; a wildie, just scraping into double figures at 10¾lb. Yet I'd always been the one who thought that wildies couldn't scrap!

Minutes after sacking this fish all hell broke loose again and I became attached to another aquatic rocket. It fought just as hard, and just as long. They were like two peas in a pod.

Talking about the fish afterwards Brian reckoned that a brace of double-figure wildies was twice as rare as a brace of 20lb mirrors. At the time of the captures, though, all he could muster was, "Oh, you lucky fellow!" Or words to that effect. Later in the week, and on subsequent visits, I was to catch a number of double-figure commons which, although lean, still bore the characteristic shape of the king carp strain.

One of the wildies going back. I had always thought the stories of their power were old wives' tales but this fish upheld the reputation!

Yes, there's no doubt about it, big wildies can scrap, and just recounting this tale has made me want a bit more of that. To echo the words of the late Bill Keal, those fish I caught that morning were wild.

"Wild? They were hopping mad."

Last Month's TV

The original Coarse Fisherman article introduced the chapter that follows with the following words: "This month the lunatic mind of Rod Hutchinson embarks on a journey to Fantasy Island. Since starting his own business just over a year ago he has now developed delusions of grandeur. This month 'This is Your Life'; next month it could be 'How I led Grimsby Town to the FA Cup'. Is Hutchinson becoming another of angling's casualties we ask ourselves?" There's no answer to that!

We all know there is too little angling on TV, and as we know many readers cannot get Angola Television on their sets we thought we'd reproduce the transcripts of one of their programmes that involved a well-known angling personality.

The scene is a crowded theatre in the middle of London. The hall is in darkness and the audience sits buzzing with excitement. A spotlight suddenly picks out a figure on the stage. Although he is dressed in silk shirt and Saville Row suit the audience is left in no doubt about his lack of upbringing. Little things like his trousers being tucked in his wellies give him away. Under his arm he carries a leatherbound Big Red Book. Moving awkwardly, as though unsure of what he should be doing, he makes his way to the microphone. Putting a finger to his lips a hush falls over the audience.

"Ladies and gentlemen, my name is Eamon Eno's and tonight we're here to pay tribute to someone I've never heard of, but, as I'm paid a fortune for doing this, who cares anyway? Now any moment the spotlight will dim and the theatre once more will be in darkness, but you should be able to make out a window at the back of the stage. Our subject for this evening has been fed false information and he believes that is the window to an office in which stands a safe containing Fred Wilton's bait recipes."

The audience gasps in disbelief. Eamon Eno's continues.

"If our research is correct it is only a matter of time before that window will open and in will climb tonight's surprise guest."

Suddenly there is a noise at the window as a ladder grates along the window ledge. The audience tenses as Eamon lets out a knowing plastic smile in their direction, and then moves into position behind the curtains as the lights dim. The window creaks as a crowbar is forced between the window and the frame. Suddenly it is forced open and in climbs a figure dressed all in black, a balaclava over his head. He walks towards the safe, pulling off his headgear in the process. Momentarily he's blinded as the house lights are switched on. He freezes in fear as Eno's steps forward from behind the curtain.

"Yes, you came here tonight believing you were going to get your hands on Fred Wilton's bait recipes, but no, it was all an elaborate plan to get you here."

Eno's suddenly realises that all is not well.

"Hang on a second, you're not our subject. Who on earth are you?"

"I'm Dick..." answers the unknown person; but before he can even get out his second name Eno's jumps in.

"Well Dirty Dick we happen to be waiting for someone special, so do you mind clearing off? Go on, on yer bike mate!"

Knowing he's obviously not wanted the relieved Dick disappears through the window. Eno's turns his attention back to the audience.

"I'm sorry about that, ladies and gentlemen, just a slight hitch. I'm sure our subject will be along at any moment."

He returns to his original position, and once more the house lights dim. Eno's gaze returns to the window as he nonchalantly picks his nose to pass the time. Within minutes the now familiar sound of a ladder on the sill is heard. Eno's creeps forward and stands beside the window. He peers down at the figure climbing the ladder. Suddenly he lifts the window, as if fuelled by temper.

"Not now Duncan, clear off, we're waiting for someone."

"Oh, very sorry old chap, I didn't know," the unseen Duncan replies.

Eno's closes the window and returns to his former position. The minutes pass and the audience starts getting restless, shuffling around in their seats from one cheek to the other. Another ladder is heard at the window. Again Eno's moves forward to the side of the window. A knowing smile lets the audience know that tonight's subject has finally arrived. Once more the window rises and a camouflaged figure falls through onto the floor. He picks himself up and ambles towards the wall, knocking a table over in the process. His back is to the audience as the lights suddenly go up. He freezes, hands up against the wall as if expecting to be searched.

"OK guv, I'll come quietly. It's a fair cop," the figure says without looking behind him.

Eno's steps forward.

"No, I'm not the police. This was all an elaborate plan to get you here tonight because, Rod Hutchinson, failed author and article writer, former trench digger and female impersonator, scaffolder of no standing and Chairman of the 'Up Yours Mate Society', this is your life."

The members of the audience look at each other puzzled, asking "Who?" of one another. Eno's leads the subject towards a chair on the left of the stage and makes him sit by giving him a sharp whack on the backside, as you would a dog. The audience now get their first real look at the victim for the evening. He has a large mop of unruly hair which looks as though it has been carefully combed with a yard brush. He carries with him two large bags – one under each eye! The eyes themselves have more red lines than a Collins road map and surely betray a weakness for alcohol. His nose is slightly upturned, an involuntary response to smelling too many baits. The backs of his hands are covered in cuts and scars from trying out his hooks for sharpness. His clothes betray a touch of class in his background: he surely bought them from a posh Oxfam shop. His feet are covered by muddy slippers in which holes have been carefully cut for air conditioning and through which his toes poke. In the house lights the audience can see a halo of midges and flies around him.

Eno's opens his Big Red Book. He has footballer's eyes, one home one away! With one on the subject and one on the audience he begins to speak.

"Yes Rod Hutchinson, you were born at a very early age in a reedbed in Norfolk. Around your neck were two labels. One read 'Not for human consumption' and the other 'Light the blue touch paper and retire immediately'. But this poor start to life did little to deter you: you were taken up by a family of water rats and treated as one of the family. It was there that you met your first childhood sweetheart and we have

her with us now, behind the curtains. Yes, it's the former Miss Deep Dyke, now working happily as a piece of chicken in a chop suey at a Chinese restaurant in Birmingham: Miss Emily Sewer Rat."

The audience applauds as a plate of chop suey is wheeled in.

"Yes," says Eno's, "after all these years it's hard for you to recognise one another."

RH says a few words to the plate but gets no reply.

"I think she's gone off me," he says. The plate is wheeled away.

Eno's continues.

"Being the quick-thinking sort of chap that you are by the age of thirteen you've realised that you aren't a rat and you depart for the city. It was there that one day you were idly going through someone's pockets when you first heard this voice."

"Hello, hello, hello, hello, hello," comes from behind the curtain.

"Yes it's the famous hiccupping copper, formerly PC Plod but now a very successful commodities broker and fence, Max Plodstein."

A huge figure with a pointed head and size fifteen feet walks through the curtains, tearing them off their rails.

"And what do you remember of the young Rod, Max?" asks Eno's.

"Well to be fair he was a bit of a tearaway when I first met him, but I soon put him on the straight and narrow. I introduced a bit of discipline into his life and belted him round the head with my truncheon ten times a day for a fortnight. I can honestly say he was in no trouble the following year."

"Why was that?" asks Eno's.

"Because he was in hospital with a fractured skull, that's why!"

The audience laughs as Plodstein makes his way to the other side of the stage, giving RH a kick in the guts on the way past, just for old time's sake. Eno's return to his Big Red Book.

"Yes, while you were in hospital you had plenty of time to think and you came out determined to make a success of your life. By the age of 26 your rise had been truly meteoric and you had your own paper round. But success in business wasn't enough and you looked for other fields in which you could use your talents. One day, while thumbing through your comics you came across a picture of a large fish. It was a carp, and although you'd never seen one before you decided there and then that one day you would catch such a fish. With your mind made up you made rapid strides and five years to the day later you caught your first carp. You're still waiting to catch your second, but that hasn't bothered you. You have risen through the ranks of the societies and today your name is revered, loathed and spat on throughout the carp world. It was at one of the early society meetings that you were first to hear this voice, which has had such a big influence on your life."

From behind the curtain a high-pitched feminine voice says:

"Hello sailor, can I show you a good time?"

RH thinks he recognises it.

"Oh, surely it's Peter?"

"No," says Eno's, "that voice which you haven't heard for fifteen years is your wife, former marine, judo black-belt and demolition worker Susan Hutchinson."

The audience applauds as a tall feline figure dressed in next to nothing and getting less all the time pounces through the curtains and starts beating Rod about the shoulders with a whip. Eno's hastily intervenes.

"And what do you remember from that first meeting?" asks Eno's of Mrs. H.

"Oh his trousers," she replies.

"What about them?" asks Eno's, puzzled.

"He didn't have any on," replies Mrs. H.

Eno's, embarrassed and colouring up, quickly ushers her away and returns to his Book.

"At the same meeting you were to get to know many carp anglers who have remained friends through all these years. One angler who was there and had no influence on you whatever is standing behind the curtain now. Do you remember this voice?"

"Jack Hilton, Fred Wilton, Bob Morris, Kevin Clifford..."

RH looks up.

"Yes, that's the old name dropper!"

"That's right you've recognised him. Failed carp fisherman, name dropper supreme, writer for obscure magazines, Matthew Black."

The curtain opens and in walks a portly figure, face hidden by straggly hair, like a Dulux Dog with glasses on. Eno's turns to him and asks:

"What do you remember about that first meeting, Matthew? What did you talk about?"

"Oh we talked for hours, Eamon, about amino acids and enzymes and proteins; or rather I talked for hours and hours about amino acids, enzymes and proteins. Rod just sat there looking bored and ignoring me."

Meanwhile RH sits in his chair, scratching his crotch, seemingly unaware of Matthew's presence. By the time Matthew has finished plugging every book he's ever read, the Carp Society and dropped a dozen more names the audience has nodded off. Eamon drops his Big Red Book on the floor with a loud bang to wake them up. Matthew is ushered away, struggling, while in mid-sentence. He tries to strike up a conversation with PC Plodstein about the molecular structure of cellulose and the associated enzymes needed for its digestion. Plodstein ignores him at first then, realising that he won't shut up, gives him a quick elbow in the throat. MB slumps to the floor gasping for air like a fish out of water. Everyone ignores him.

Eno's returns to his Big Red Book.

"Unbeknown to you at that same meeting, lying beneath a table with his head stuck in a bag of glue, was someone who would hold back your writing for the next ten years. Do you remember this voice?"

A voice from behind the curtain says:

"Your cheque's in the post."

"Yes, it's that well-known writer of particularly nasty columns, poser at matches and star-maker David Small."

In through the curtains ambles a swaying figure, obviously three sheets to the wind and doing little twirls in the process to advertise his Barbour jacket.

"Yes David," says Enos, "you were one of the first to spot Rod's literary talents, yet it was many years after starting your magazine that you were to use one of his articles. Was there a reason for that?"

"Yes Eamon, in a word, money. He wanted paying, which is against my policy. If I paid him God knows where it would end. I might have to pay them all."

David makes his way to his seat, flashing the label of his coat in the process.

"The following year," Eamon resumes, "your career took what looked to be a serious setback when, due to the strain of waiting for cheques that were in the post you suffered a mental breakdown. You were admitted to a home for mental defectives. This experience, which could have left serious scars on you for life surprisingly turned out to be a huge stroke of luck. For also locked in that home were the committee members of one of the country's best-known carp syndicates and in no time at all you had grovelled your way in. From that point onwards your career progressed in leaps and bounds and in 1975 you managed a feat unprecedented in carp fishing. In that year you fished twenty different waters containing twenty pounders, and blanked on all of them. Not content with that feat you then fished fifteen different waters containing thirties, and blanked on all of them, too. No wonder you acquired the tag 'Mr. Consistency'!"

"At one of these lakes a young action man introduced you to a revolutionary new way of acquiring huge catches. The method was simple. Think of a number, double it, then multiply it by four and the figure you arrived at was the sum total of the fish caught that year. No wonder huge catches were soon amassed."

"Yes, with the years of experience mounting up and all the knowledge of new techniques you had acquired your career was surely heading for a new pinnacle. And so it proved when on 16th June 1980, after twenty years of endeavour, you finally achieved what many thought was impossible. Using specially designed rods and reels and a 200% protein, multi-enzyme hormone based particle bait you caught your second carp."

"Yes, tonight we are proud to say, Rod Hutchinson, This is Your Life."

A Day in the Life...

I got home at 2.00 p.m. having driven like a madman, as usual. The GPO was due at four o'clock to pick up three days-worth of mail order. Two hours to make up 33 parcels. I knew I'd never do it. The phone never stopped ringing. I shouldn't moan; the baits were taking off in a big way. Everyone wants Seafoodblend. I know the others are just as good. I try to explain that to the customers, but no, it's Seafood and Minglefruit (the most expensive two to produce are the ones they want!). Somehow – I don't know how – I got the orders done. I even had the postman weighing them up for me. I could do with Sue here to help, but she's tanning her belly on some Spanish beach, mosquitoes and local Lotharios sniffing round for the kill.

In the middle of the paperwork involved with the postman the phone shrieks again. I try to ignore it, but then realise that it might be a shop re-ordering for my house. I'm into the bank manager, for my house, socks and underpants (he's funny that way). I'd better answer it and get rid of the stuff.

"Hello, is that Rod Hutchinson?"

"No, this is his brother Arnold. Can I help?"

"Actually you probably can. Is it true that Rod is using Algerian fish oil in his Seafoodblend?"

"I don't know, but I do know he's spent his holidays in Morocco the past couple of years. Is that any help to you?"

"Yes, thank you very much. That can explain a lot."

I put the phone down. The orders are away: into the garage to pick up some casein. I'm two weeks behind on orders, having run out: got to get the bloody stuff packed. I've spent so many hours here in the garage in the past few months I'm due for a service.

8.00 p.m. and I've got 100 bags packed, I'm head to foot in dust like a Homepride flour grader. I jump into the bath and protein scum floats around the edges. The damn phone rings again and again I try to ignore it, but it keeps ringing. I charge downstairs starkers.

"Hello!" I shout at the other end hoping they'll put the phone down. It is some idiot talking in a false German accent about my bait. I bawl 'Heil Hitler' down the phone and hang up. Run upstairs, jump back into the bath, lay back, put a tape on, smoke my pipe and survey my prospects floating in the scum. Ring, ring, ring – the wretched phone again! I give up. Down the stairs, bedraggled, dripping water everywhere: it's a friend from down south.

"Expect Hans, one of the biggest wholesalers in Germany to ring you. I've had a good talk with him and he wants to wholesale your bait through the Common Market."

"Can you excuse me for just a moment please?" I ask, "I'm just going to slit my throat."

I gave up on the bath and was lying on the settee watching Seb Coe running on TV when there is a knock at the door. I answer it, completely forgetting I'm starkers. It's the paper girl. Well I'm not flashing with a body like mine so I cover my embarrassment, pay her and send her on her way.

Eleven o'clock. I'm laid back with my feet up on a chair cooling out in the village pub. I feel good; all orders away and things are ticking over nicely. Plus I'm catching some good fish. Yesterday I fluked another thirty. I don't know why it happens to me but it does and I hope it never rubs off. I remember the words of a Norfolk friend of mine:

"There are good anglers, and there are lucky anglers, and if you are lucky you don't need to be good."

I bet Brian would agree with those sentiments.

I'm tired. I was up at five this morning. The beer has gone to my head, legs, bladder, and socks (I missed the toilet). I walk out of the pub. A warm wind hits me in the face. It's a belter. I'd been praying for one like this earlier in the week when I was fishing. Walking in that sideways, crab-like motion I always do when leaving a pub the old box is working overtime. The wind will be blowing straight into my favourite swim down at the local lake. I was in no state to drive. I stumbled down the bank at 1.30 a.m. It's pitch black and I can't see a thing. Pressing the rod rest in it hits a soft spot. The rest disappears and I follow it into the lake.

I don't know what happened next: it is a complete blackout. All I know is that I woke up at 4.00 a.m., teeth chattering away faster than a 'mother-in-law meets the wife' movie and alongside my head is a reel handle spinning like crazy! That much I have since recalled. When I awoke the second time, around five, it was to discover the rods all over and a sack in the margins. I was lost as to the reasons. The weight I daren't mention. All I can do is repeat my friend's wisdom: "There are good anglers and lucky anglers, and it is better to be lucky".

I should add to that philosophy that although the lucky ones don't look as though they are trying in their own way they put in a lot of effort. For instance I once put a pint down to get back to the lake. Only once mind!

I fell through the door at 6.00 a.m. completely shattered. I woke at 8.00 a.m. to find myself laid on the bed fully clothed with some idiot banging on the door. It was the postman with a recorded delivery that had to be signed for.

"I've been hoping to have a word with you," he says. "Do you sell big treble hooks? Me and my mate go fishing for salmon. Well it's not fishing really, we foul hook them!"

"I'm sorry, I don't sell trebles. There is a tackle dealer at Gainsborough who stocks game tackle and treble hooks."

"Thanks a lot," says the postman, "I'll go and see him."

He hands me another dozen orders. Two hours later I've done them and collapse on the floor. The next time I wake it is to a banging on the window. It is some bloke who has come to buy some bait. I recognise him immediately...

Earlier in the season Brian and I had a day on a small private syndicate lake of which this chap was a member. Without wishing to appear rude not many of the members had a clue. They'd obtained a lake which just happened to be full of carp, a species about which they knew very little. On that day carp were practically crawling up the bank in their spawning activities. The lake was a mass of foam as the carp tore up and down, crashing through any reeds and weed that got in their way. Around midday I had noticed this gentleman stomping the margins, every few minutes plunging his landing net in the direction of spawning carp. My curiosity got the better of me so I went round and asked him just what he was doing.

"I'm trying to net the carp, mate," he said.

"Whatever for?" asked I.

"So I can milk them," he replied.

"Don't you think that's a bit dangerous?" I asked.

He looked at me puzzled.

"No son, they don't bite you know."

He was soon served. I snoozed, the phone rang again. Life goes on...

Woldview

Walking out knee-deep in mud along the cattle-trodden path that led to the Wood Farm dairy I had this most extraordinary feeling of mixed emotions. On the one hand I had secured a long-term lease on a water over which I had complete control, something I had always dreamed of. On the other hand I had that feeling you have after a meeting with the bank manager: it was as if I'd been mentally mugged.

Quentin the old farmer who owned the lake had no problems with me taking over the water, but I had to sort out the financial aspects of the lease with his wife Grace. Now Grace was a lovely lady and a canny Scot at the same time. In negotiations she drove a very hard bargain. Not only had I agreed to pay twice as much for the lease as I knew I could get back from a syndicate but after Grace had learnt that I had once been a landscape gardener I had also agreed to redesign her garden and lay it out for her! On top of that I had to stock the water as it had no fish in it other than a handful of trout she had stocked for her relatives to fish for, and several million sticklebacks. The more I thought about it the more obvious it became that my bait company, which was going well at the time, would have to subsidise the lake for at least three years, by which time I could hopefully turn it into a thriving carp water. Before that time swims had to be built as two of the three banks on the triangular-shaped lake were perpendicular to the water. In addition trees, shrubs and water plants had to be introduced to make a good environment not only for the fish and the wildlife, but also for prospective syndicate members.

Turning the water into a carp lake was a true labour of love. I had spent the previous fifteen years of my life travelling to pastures far afield in an effort to catch carp larger than those we had in Lincolnshire at that time. This was my chance to have big fish in my own back yard.

In retrospect the hardest part was building the swims and getting any sort of vegetation growing around the lake. All the top soil had been taken off and redeposited on the top of the bottom lake, which had been filled in and reclaimed. What I was left with was pure sand. Practically everything I planted just withered away and died. There were simply no nutrients in the soil and any rain or moisture promptly ran through it like a dose of salts. After the first year I seriously wondered if I could ever turn it into anything resembling a carp lake. That was until one night I had a bit of luck and a raffle ticket I had purchased in the pub nearest the lake came up. This was no ordinary prize! In aid of the Air Ambulance a local farmer had donated a tanker full of pig slurry.

**Converting the bare banks from a barren waste to an
attractive natural environment was a frustrating labour of love.**

My first thought was:

"What on earth am I going to do with that?!"

But thinking about it I realised that it was full of nitrogen with some phosphate traces and I soon persuaded the farmer to spray it onto the banks around the lake. During the winter it smelt absolutely foul but by the following spring everything was blooming and for the first time you could see the future shape of the lake taking place. It was no longer just a hole in the ground with water in it.

It may surprise anyone who sees the water today to know that all the various reeds around the water were planted. My friend Malcolm (Charlie) Besson was a keen gardener. He split all the plants around his garden pond and planted them around the lake. He is responsible for the wonderful show of marsh marigolds which bloom around the islands in spring. Most of the reeds are down to Robbo, a carp angler from my then-home village of Marshchapel. He was digging up all manner of reeds and grasses from the dykes close to our homes and

The changing face of the shallows at Woldview over the years.

transplanting them into the margins of the lake. That first year I only had eight members, and two of those were from far away, yet everyone did their bit in either planting, or digging swims.

Obtaining stock was no problem, other than that the fish stocked were small and would take between three and five years to grow to a suitable size for a syndicate to fish for. I had been writing for Angling Times and one day got a call from a Mr. Thomas who at that time was Estate Manager for Elsham Hall Country Park, which was only some twenty minutes drive from the lake. Mr. Thomas had a problem. There were two lakes on the estate. The top lake was exclusive for trout fishing. The bottom lake was full of carp which could be fed by the public from a small jetty which jutted out from the bank. Although not much more than an acre this lake held an incredible number of carp to over twenty pounds. In the wild the biomass of the water would have been impossible to emulate but because the fish were being fed regularly by the public they were thriving. There was also a smaller water, the Ornamental or Duck Lake. Although tiny at just quarter of an acre maximum this fenced-off water was the home of exotic ducks which had been flown in at great expense as a feature for the public to watch, feed and photograph.

Mr. Thomas had two major problems, the first being that carp had got into the Trout Lake and were clouding up the water as they burrowed through the silt in search of food. As a consequence the trout couldn't see the anglers' flies. Returns from the anglers were very poor and he was losing members.

His second problem was that carp had also got into his exotic Duck Pond. As a result it was impossible to grow pond weeds, which are food for the ducks, because the carp kept tearing them up. He had tried netting with fyke nets, normally used for netting eels, but all to no avail. Could I help him? Could I give him any advice? I replied that I could sort his problem out, but only by using rod and line. He couldn't believe it. He had read old books in the past saying that carp were impossible to catch but took my word for it that I could do the job he

Bob Jones with what I believe may have been the first twenty caught from Woldview.

desired. No money was to change hands but I could – indeed had to – take away any carp I caught! From having no stock at all I suddenly had the potential to have more carp than I could handle.

But there again my first trip to the Trout Lake did not go as I had expected. I crept in through the walled garden that surrounded the lake about an hour after dawn and was promptly ambushed by about

Yours truly with the first 20lb+ common to be caught from the syndicate lake.

a dozen peacocks which expected to be fed every time they saw a member of the public. The pet llama also seemed to have the same expectations. The noise they all set off was incredible and must have woken everyone within a five-mile radius. All I could do was feed them my sandwiches and get the hell out of there!

The carp in the Trout Lake had never been fished for so there was only one plan of attack: virgin fish are suckers for sweetcorn. I catapulted a tin into what appeared to be clouded-up water then cast out two grains on the hook over the free offerings. Before it hit the bottom the line screamed off. It was a trout of about two pounds! Six trout later I was beginning to think that the Estate Manager would not be too impressed by my efforts and might think that I was poaching his trout. A change of tactics was called for. By this time there were plenty of members of staff milling round the gardens watering the plants, feeding the animals, filling the carp and duck feed dispensers and so on. Luckily a simple change to floating crust resulted in me catching three carp up to 14lb inside an hour, and all in front of the staff. The Estate Manager was well impressed by my results.

Over the course of the summer I was able to put 36 carp into Woldview from the Trout and Duck Lakes, 32 of which were common carp. I could have stocked twice as many fish but didn't want Woldview to be a predominantly commons water. I was seeking a healthy balance between commons and mirrors and, hopefully, leather carp. But the Elsham fish really proved their value when a fishery manager I knew wanted to convert his lake from a specimen water into a match lake. As tends to be the case with these types of lakes it only held a fraction of the number of big carp the owner believed it held but I was happy to exchange 25 three to eight pound carp for four mirror carp weighing from 20lb to 24lb.

Meanwhile a couple of syndicate members who fished the River Trent were also dropping any nice mirrors they might catch into Woldview, quite legally by the rules of the time. By the end of the first year's lease I had a good healthy stock of carp which would hopefully thrive. Because I knew what had gone into the water – after all I had caught the majority of the fish once already – I made a personal decision not to fish the lake for three years although I was paying for its lease. I just wanted to let the fish grow on. Hopefully by the time I caught them again I wouldn't be able to recognise them.

Woldview was up and running.

By dawn Roger Smith had joined the Woldview Twenties club!

Although other members had fished Woldview before I did so only single and double figure fish had been caught prior to my first session three years after the water was stocked. On that first session I was accompanied by my good friends Roger Smith and Bob Jones (not the Bob Jones from the Redmire Syndicate!) from the Savay syndicate. As was our usual way we got our bivvies and beds sorted out, hookbaits tied on and hooked into the butt ring ready to cast

out, and swims baited heavily before we retired – first of all to the pub and then to the fish and chip shop. This arrangement wasn't merely to refresh ourselves but also to allow the swims to settle down after the bombardment of bait.

An hour after we returned and cast out a buzzer sounded and minutes later Bob called, "I've got one." Ten minutes later one of my rods shot off and I was soon yelling, "I've got one, too!" Then, just before dawn, Roger's alarm broke the peace and tranquillity and it wasn't long before he was calling across, "I've got one, too!"

At dawn it transpired that we had all caught twenties. Mine was a common while Bob and Roger's fish were mirrors. Woldview was well and truly on its way to being the top carp water I had dreamed of creating when I had first rented it as a hole in the ground with water in it!

Big Un

When the weather is right there is no place on earth I would rather be than Lincolnshire. It was a hot afternoon: English hot and bearable. There was a caressing breeze gently massaging my skin under the hot afternoon sun. Mad Tim, who lived on the lake, had been round a couple of hours earlier to force-feed me a couple of cans of McEwan's Export. I didn't need them but joined in with him just to be friendly. I had a nice glow on.

Mad Tim, who lived on the lake, had been round a couple of hours earlier.

The combination of the sun, the couple of beers, and the warm breeze blowing in my face gradually seeped through my defences and I drifted off into the land of Nod. In my head was an automatic alarm clock. Castle Lake was less than a mile from the sea. As the tide came in the breeze would pick up and the carp would follow it all the way down behind the island where I was waiting to intercept them. All around the margins of the island it was relatively shallow and the warm rays from the sun made it perfect for surface fishing, the lapping waves invigorating the surface layers with intoxicating oxygen. I knew from the hours I had spent on the water that it was just a matter of time before one of the many carp, following each other like a procession, would make a mistake and take my floating bait. Despite the waves and the glare from the sun I could make out the large shapes eyeing up my floating morsels like sharks beneath a mackerel shoal. At any moment one of the two hookbaits I had out among them was sure to be taken.

My rods were set up by the water's edge while I was lying on the sloping sand bank some twenty feet away in order not to cast a shadow across the water. The breeze was northeasterly, pushing through the channel between the bank and island to my right, but pushing my baits to my left towards the bay, which was flat and calm. But something

"Out of ten I'd have given her fifteen and a half." Big Dave's wife Jane in the Lido days of the early Eighties.

in my peripheral vision to the right caught my eye. I watched her move along the shoreline, slowly, gracefully, stopping now and then, dipping her toes in the water, then tossing her hair in the breeze like a flamingo preening herself. I watched her every move, which wasn't easy considering my head was facing in the opposite direction. She moved onwards along my bank and when she encountered my rods she moved up the bank between the rods and me. She was beautiful with lovely sun-bleached tousled hair and beautiful golden skin, and as she passed by she glanced over her shoulder, giving me a cheeky little smile. It was just like that scene from the Dudley Moore/Bo Derek film 'Ten'. Out of ten I'd have given her fifteen and a half! As she moved along the bank on that glorious afternoon I just couldn't take my eyes off her.

Suddenly, from nowhere, the sky went black; an unexpected total eclipse of the sun. I looked up at the sky and made out the frame of the biggest creature I had ever seen. It was terrifying, half Incredible Hulk, half Yorkie! It was my worst nightmare. Not only could he swot me like a fly and crumble my bones in his fingers, I also knew that I could never win an argument with him. Then the voice came, roaring like an avalanche down a mountainside.

"You!"

I tried to make out that I hadn't noticed him.

You! I hope you weren't eyeing up our Myrtle?"

Taking a big gulp of air I stuttered:

"No mate, I was watching my floater. It's just here, by the island. Can you see it?" I asked, pointing towards it.

At that moment a carp came up and took it, in all probability saving my life. The ensuing fight broke the tension and after five minutes or so Big Un netted a big double for me. He even took a couple of photos of me posing with my saviour fish, by which time his Myrtle had joined him.

That was my introduction to big Dave Walker and his wife Jane. In the north of England Sheffield is known as the City of Seven Hills.

He even took a couple of photos of me posing with my saviour fish...

Dave is one of them.

After that fateful day back in the early Eighties we all became friends and Dave and I fished together many times. There have been a few adventures both on and away from the lakes and as yet I've got away without being terminally swatted – although there were a couple of occasions when I came perilously close!

One was on another hot afternoon down at Castle Lake. It was a bank holiday and the lake was packed with tourists and campers. We'd had a bit of a party at my house the night before and besides Dave and a few locals some friends we had met in Kent had come up for the do, all taking their turns at the sound system. No one had gone to sleep before dawn and when we woke all and sundry were hung over and tired as newts. Our southern friends left just after midday in an effort to beat the bank holiday traffic. Dave, the other local lads and I decided

The crowds gathered to watch Dave's capture of
the Lido's big un and the photo session that followed.

to go for a walk around Castle Lake, just for some fresh air. We had no intentions of fishing.

At that time Castle was the jewel of the Lincolnshire carp lakes and was a secret to all but a few in the know. Consequently with it being packed out with trippers we didn't all want to be seen fishing or it would have been only a matter of time before someone put two and two together. We had made the right choice because one of the first people we bumped into on our walk was a well-known Nottingham carp angler out for a day at the coast with his family. With the heat and sunshine many of the day trippers took to pedaloes which were available for hire and were happily making their way up and down the lake. I had seen it before: the oxygen created by the pedaloes got the carp feeding and by mid afternoon they were crashing between the boats.

"Come on," said Dave, "let's get the rods out."

"No," said I, "it's too easy. We're bound to catch and that would blow the water."

"Well I'm fishing," said Dave, "and that's that!"

And that was that: after all who was going to stop him? Not me, that's for sure, but I have to admit I had the right hump with him.

Sure enough, first cast out between the boats, the bait had only just hit bottom when "Weeee", the buzzer screamed and he was in. Within seconds there was a big crowd of day trippers standing behind him on the high bank, watching the action. To give him his due he played the fish expertly between the boats, those on board seemingly unaware of what was happening. Minutes later, gritting my teeth with anger, I slipped the net beneath a big mirror. It only happened to be the biggest fish in the lake, weighing 28lb, all this happening in front of a crowd bigger than my beloved Grimsby Town drew on a Saturday afternoon!

There must have been fifty cameras flashing away at him as he posed with his prize. He was happy, without a doubt, but he made one vital mistake.

"Grief it's hot," he said, sweat running down his face.

That was it. Behind him was a bucket with a few baits in it. I tipped them out, filled it with water and from the back tipped the water over his head. He was still holding the fish and could do nothing about it. I beat a hasty retreat, legging it into the nearby pine woods while he cooled off. Luckily for me in the fierce heat his clothes soon dried out – and he caught another fish – so by the time we met up again he had calmed down a bit. Not that he has ever forgotten the incident, and he frequently reminds me that he'll get me back one day.

Now for some reason, probably because Dave is a fair few years younger than me, I would often refer to him as 'son.'

"All right son?" I'd ask.

"All right dad," he'd reply, which I preferred to 'old timer,' which he occasionally used.

Be that as it may our usual greeting once got me out of a bit of a scrape. It was a weekend again and we'd had a good morning on Castle, taking quite a few fish. By early afternoon the lake had gone flat calm and the carp had stopped feeding so the few of us on the lake, me, Big Dave, Gary Bayes and the two Market Rasen lads Bonk and Longpocket decided to go to the local pub for a pool challenge. It was going to be a pound each into the kitty, winner to take the lot – although we couldn't prise more than fifty pence out of Longpocket!

We tossed up as to who would start. I won, then the challenger would pay for the game – so on and so on, with the winner staying on. First up it was me and Gary Bayes. After a close game, during which we both managed to pot more whites than we did colours, I managed to nick it – by default I might add as Gary potted the black, closely followed by the white.

As we got another pint in the tranquil atmosphere was shattered by the sound of 'Vrooom, vroom...' and the smell of petrol and oil wafted in through the open door. It was the local biker gang from Mablethorpe, many of whom I knew, most of them being a great bunch of lads. In my younger days I'd been a biker myself but had given it up for fear of

I was a biker at one time – but kept falling off – so I knew most of the bikers who interrupted our afternoon game of pool.

serious injury after falling off too many times. I made the usual small talk with those of the lads I knew, the usual stuff like asking what they were riding, and did old so-and-so still have his Bonneville? It was just the stuff bikers talk about, then I made my way back to the pool table.

"Right, who's on next?" I asked across the table.

"I am," said one of the Rasen lads.

"Then it's me," said the other.

"No you're not," came the snarling voice of a big burly bloke who had come in with the biker boys.

"I'm on next!"

He looked a real handful and nasty with it. Sensibly the Rasen boys backed down. Not that they were averse to a scrap or two but judging by the lumps, bumps and black eyes that they seemed permanently to carry they obviously weren't much good at it. Rumour had it that only a fortnight earlier they had come out of their local village boozer, out of their heads, picked a fight with a scarecrow, and had taken a right hammering! When it came to a fight they were about as useful as a pair of PVA underpants are to a man with the dribbles.

Now I'm not a great pool player but I was far better than Mr. Nasty and soon saw him off. "Best of three," he said, stamping his hand on the table. No problem: another game, same result, only this time I seven-balled him, meaning that he didn't put a ball down, only the white – on numerous occasions! As he walked from the table, steam coming out of his ears, in walked Big Dave. He was a bit late, having gone to their caravan to collect Jane.

"Am I on yet?" enquired Dave, checking to see it if was his turn on the table yet.

"No, you're arm wrestling with me," snarled the fuming voice of Mr. Nasty. Jane turned to me with a worried look on her face.

"Please don't let him get into trouble Rod," she said concernedly.

"You OK with that, son?" I called to Dave.

"I'll give it a go dad," replied Dave with a shrug of his shoulders.

Soon the arms were locked and everyone in the pub crowded round, watching. Mr. Nasty was all pumped up, muscles bulging, veins as prominent as a motorway on a road map, sweat dripping down his brow. Dave, meanwhile, appeared to be taking it all lightheartedly. Jane's words were ringing in my ears, "Please don't let him get into trouble," but if Dave couldn't handle the situation what chance did I have?

Meanwhile Mr. Nasty was letting out primeval grunts while Dave sat there as cool as a cucumber. After two or three minutes Dave asked when they were going to start.

"We have started," snarled the nasty one, putting in one almighty effort, trying to catch Dave off guard. Dave acted as if nothing had happened then slowly, irreversibly, pushed his adversary's arm to the table. The nasty one once more demanded the best of three. It was the same result again, only this time Dave smacked the bloke's fist hard into the table. By now Mr. Nasty was getting really cross and demanded that they should now use their other arm. Now this was a big mistake to make as he hadn't realised that Dave had used his weaker arm first! Dave slammed Mr. Nasty's fist down so hard on the table that I swear you could hear the shattering of knuckles. Not surprisingly this time Mr. Nasty didn't demand the best of three.

The crowd dispersed around the pub while the nasty one sat at his table alone, huffing and puffing and nursing his knuckles. The conflict appeared to be over and I returned to our pool game. Tranquillity was restored.

"You're next son," I said to Dave.

"OK dad," he replied, setting the balls up.

But the nasty one hadn't finished.

"You!" he yelled across the room. We all ignored him.

"You!" he yelled again, pointing at me. "It's your turn."

I sauntered across to him in what I hoped came across as a relaxed manner.

"Sit down," he said, "it's your turn."

I leant over and replied:

"Look mate, the day you can beat my lad you can take me on. Until then I suggest you go and practice up the nurses' home."

With that he slammed his glass down, told the other bikers to drink up, and stormed out of the door.

By the way, to make his day complete 'my lad' stuffed me at pool.

Jane wasn't her usual self that following summer. She was broody and wanted to start a family. I'm not sure that Dave was too keen at the time, wanting to get financially set up before they had children, but as is always the outcome in my experience women always get their way in these matters. What would we do without them, bless 'em? Not too long after little John Walker appeared, and not too long after that followed the lovely Katie. The years passed and the children seemed to grow faster than sunflowers. In no time at all they were young people, each displaying traits of both their parents.

John's school was engaged in a student exchange scheme with other schools across Europe. As part of the scheme Jane and the big fella agreed to take in a student from Germany. Now Dave can be very forthright and outspoken at times – like every time he opens his mouth, for instance – while Jane, for the most part, plays it prim and proper. For a month before the student arrived Jane, in true Fawlty Towers mode, was driving it into Dave:

"Whatever you do don't mention the war."

Dave with his dry wit would generally make some sort of riposte, but Jane was adamant.

"Don't you mention the war or I'll never speak to you again, and your rations will be cut off!"

Dave realised how serious his good lady was about this and duly took heed, vowing to be on his best behaviour.

Cometh the hour and the day and the said student arrived. As he had promised Dave was as good as gold, although the slight trickle of blood emanating from his lips revealed just how hard he was biting his tongue. Jane was the perfect hostess, as anyone who knows her would expect, laying on their usual evening meal, thinking the boy would be hungry. It was nothing posh; the usual sauerkraut, veiner schnitzel and a variety of spicy sausages. After the evening meal they all sat around talking, Jane wanting to know all about Germany and the town the boy lived in.

"I have many photographs with me if you would like to see them," said the boy.

Jane replied that she would love to see them.

After browsing through the photographs Jane turned to the boy expressing her surprise that the town was so modern, and that most of the buildings looked relatively new. From the little she had read up on the town it was a site of German architectural heritage.

"Oh it was like that," replied the student, "but the English bombed it flat in the war."

"I think it's time we went to bed now, Mrs. Fawlty," said Dave to Jane, "the boy must be tired from all the travelling he has done."

Flashback to the Castle years...

Dave really is a big un! Here he is pictured with mere
mortals at Darenth Tip Lake in the early Eighties.
Bill Walford, on the left of the group is over six feet tall!

When we had a party on a Saturday night we would lay on an open buffet with buns, hams, cheese, butter, pork pies, quiche, egg custards, pies and so on, all from the bakery in Louth, a true connoisseur's butchers and bakery. There was more than enough for everyone but the usual suspects, Longpocket and his chum, would rush through to the kitchen and stuff themselves like hamsters, cheeks bulging, gloating, almost proud of the fact that they had filled their bellies without spending a penny. After the hamsters had left others would drift through, putting a bit of whatever they fancied on their plate.

I was in no hurry, there was plenty of food and I could wait until the gannets had had their fill. Once the kitchen was more or less empty I made my way through. Myrtle was in the kitchen selectively picking out her food, like ladies do: nothing fattening mind, a little bit of quiche, a slice of ham, a few pickles, and a noggin of cheese. She was looking after her figure and was positively glowing. That morning she had announced to us that she was pregnant for the first time. Myrtle was a very happy lady and with catching the sun that day she had a golden aura about her. I couldn't help it: I just burst into song with an old Frankie Vallee hit:

"My eyes adore you,

Though I've never laid a hand on you,

My eyes adore..."

As I was singing the jolly green giant walked into the kitchen, catching me mid serenade. I froze on the spot expecting finally to be swatted. All I could say was:

"Sorry son, I couldn't help myself."

"That's all right old timer; I thought you were singing to the pork pie. By the way you were out of tune."

With that he picked up a large pork pie and consumed it in two bites! Good on yer, Big Un.

A Cappella
(Unaccompanied)

Falling in love and walking into marriage are the easiest things in the world; it's a breeze. There is so much to look forward to. There are the stag and hen parties, the wedding itself, the reception, and the disco after: all things that have to be organised, but fun at the same time. In addition, if you are lucky, you have the prospect of getting your leg over twice a month for the foreseeable future.

Seriously, I love weddings; I just seem to be allergic to my own. All the girls are excited, getting their outfits ready for the big day. All the kids are excited, getting measured for their bridesmaids' dresses. It's an exciting time for everyone, and the only reservation I have is that the bridesmaids' dresses seem to have been made by a lady usually employed making industrial curtains. Even the blokes get up for it, all being measured up at Guy the Tailor for their wedding suits. I was in there myself getting measured up. Having sorted out the colour, material, price and all that stuff I was shown into a booth for the intimate measurements.

"Would you like us to concentrate on any particular aspect of your body sir? Is there any aspect you would like us to enhance?"

I was lost for words but he was well into his salesman's spiel.

"You have big shoulders sir; we could accentuate them, which would make your waist look much slimmer. And a lot of you young virile guys like us to concentrate on the crotch area, to make them look extremely well hung," then, after having a quick feel round the said area continued, "although that would be very difficult in your case, sir."

I was trying to think of a witty response to that one when my blushes were spared by another customer and another assistant going into the booth next to the one I was in. From the assistant's first words I knew it could only be Mally.

"Do you mind removing the parrot, please sir?"

The salesperson-come-fashion-consultant went through the well-rehearsed dialogue.

"Would you like us to concentrate on any particular aspect of your body sir?"

Mally stopped him in his tracks.

"Can you make my nose look smaller?"

Seriously, marriage is a day to look forward to. Coming out of a marriage when you don't want to, and don't expect to, can be devastating. I was down as a down person can be, more depressed than a soggy egg custard. I felt totally lost. All my life I'd been cradled by the family. There was always someone to talk me through whatever problems I had. For the first eighteen years of my life I'd had the protection of mam and my brothers: for the next twenty three my own wife and children (and not forgetting the dog). I couldn't understand what it was all about. One minute I was happy, contented and seemingly successful; next minute I was living on my own in a caravan. Even the dog had the hump with me. I didn't go out, didn't go fishing, did nothing. In a small community like the area I lived in everyone knows your business. Gossip is the life blood of every village post office. I couldn't handle the times I heard:

"Sorry to hear about your break up," although in reality they were asking, "Have you got any more juicy flesh to hang on the bone?"

For a few weeks I was a recluse, like Howard Hughes, but without the money! Then out of the blue one afternoon Big Un burst in, pan full of curry in one hand, six popadoms, three naan breads and four onion bhajis in the other. It was good to see him but I wished he'd opened the door first!

I loved the meal, stuffing myself to the gills. We had a few jars and just talked and reflected. First of all we talked about all the things in life of which we had some knowledge. That took about ten minutes. We fell to sleep on the things in life we did not understand; like women; like why you never see a sheep on a bicycle; like why does a woodpecker never get a headache, and like why, after being tormented for three days with a stony silence, does a woman choose to break that silence during Match of the Day? These are just a few of life's imponderables.

Anyway Dave shook me out of my despondency and invited me over to Sheffield for the weekend to stay with him and Myrtle. Dave knew my tastes in music and was going to take me to a 'cool' venue to see the new hot band in town. Sounds good doesn't it? You hear it every night in summer on the TV, young kids extolling the virtues of whatever music festival they've been assigned to. Easy peasy, but try doing it with an Arthur Scargill accent and see how far you get! Be that as it may be Dave sold me on the gig and I was looking forward to seeing Myrtle again, and their new offspring young Johnny Walker (so

Dave shook me out of my despondency and invited me over to Sheffield.

named because he was only a little tot!).

Sheffield is only sixty miles from me but it's a devilish place to find your way around. What should have been a two-hour journey took about five hours. I come from the sticks and Sheffield then was such a vibrant place, and more cosmopolitan than I had ever imagined. It was more like London in the Sixties: lots of people on the streets, colourful clothes, trendy boutiques and even wine bars. The smell of different foods and different cultures was heavy in the air of the city centre. Everywhere giant billboards advertised the city's emerging bands like Human League, ABC, Heaven Seventeen: they were the big three! The air was electric and by the time I finally found my way to Big Un's house I'd been garlanded with rose petals, joined the Black Dyke Brass Band fan club and become a full card-carrying member of the Communist Party!

I'd lost my voice as well. All the way across I'd been singing at the top of my voice, the thought of Myrtle filling my head.

"I drove all night, to get to you,
Was that all right?"
And the other big 'un:

"Red light, green light,
Driving through the dark night,
Driving through the pouring rain,
Just got to see Jane..."

I was well up for it, but have to admit that an eerie chill went up my spine as I passed this great big smack-in-your-face sign saying proudly:

"You are now entering the Soviet Republic of South Yorkshire."

Then there was a border post where you had to show your union card. It was quoted in the Lincolnshire Tourist Guide that every summer 100,000 people from Sheffield visit Lincolnshire. It would have been twice that number but the average Sheffield citizen can't find their way out of the place! But it's a cool city; downright freezing, in fact, most times I visit it!

Anyway I made it: Myrtle gave me the kick up the arse advice I needed, and it was off into the lights of the big city with Big Un, the sun-bleached kid as my escort.

I don't know where in the city Dave took me, but it was good. There was a really laid-back atmosphere. I seem to recall it was called 'Mr. Kite's'. The theme of the décor and the atmosphere seemed very post-war Parisian featuring Toulouse Lautrec, posters on the wall, chequered linen table cloths and Gauloise cigarettes in the vending machine. When I read the menu I was totally surprised to find that it was an Italian restaurant. But that's Sheffield for you. And me, I guess.

We arrived early, soon after seven. Already the place was filling up. Dave, either by luck or good judgement, got us a table directly opposite two pretty young ladies. After giving them the once over – come on it's a man's job to look at attractive women; part of the job description – I thought no more about it. From what I could work out through the Gauloise haze (this being in the days long before the smoking ban) they were much too young anyway for a man of my advancing years.

Over the course of the next hour the members of the band slowly made their way in, all resplendent in their baggy, shiny, Fifties-style suits, immaculate in their white silk shirts with matching ties. For anyone

A Cappella

familiar with the great rock and roll film 'The Girl Can't Help It', they looked just like the Platters. I was wondering where all the roadies were with all the equipment when in walked a guy with an acoustic Spanish-style guitar under his arm. There were no roadies and no equipment.

The band did the whole set *a cappella*. There were no mikes, just wonderful harmonies. Their numbers were all Fifties' standards, which were the hit pop songs of their day. Their interpretations and wonderful harmonies were backed by this lone acoustic guitarist who managed to sound like a whole orchestra on his own. The band, 'The Dizzy Club', was brilliant and each number seemed better than the last. Maybe that was because by this time we had consumed two bottles of wine between us, although in retrospect I must have drunk most of it as Dave was driving.

It was a really enjoyable night. When the set finished and people descended to the bar Dave mentioned to me that one of the girls opposite had been eyeing me up all night. I wondered if it was a wind up, a case of "Old Rod needs a treat"!

"Go on," he says, "go and buy her a drink, go and chat her up."

I really didn't want to know. I was just there for the music and a drink and made all manner of excuses as to why I wasn't interested. I think that somewhere along the line Dave picked me up by my belt and shirt collar and carried me across the room, picked up a chair and sat me on it next to this attractive young lady.

"Look love, this guy's been dying to talk to you all night and he'd love to come over and buy you a drink."

He turned and walked off to the bar, leaving me in limbo. If he'd been just half his size I'd have clouted him. As my relationship count goes up it shows that I'm just not very good with the opposite sex. I grew up with brothers and no sisters. I went to an all-boys school. I like girls but don't really know how to communicate with them. I've always found conversation so hard. Very few girls are into football, fishing and boxing. The occasional one is into music, but in the few experiences I have had generally the band or artist that they love is one that I loathe.

Pretty though this girl was I knew I was running out of conversation when she'd not even heard the football results! Somewhere along the line I found out that she was a thirty-year-old nurse who worked at the Royal Hallamshire in the Geriatric Unit.

"I thought I knew your face," she said, handing me a paper napkin. "My phone number's on there if ever you need us."

I wasn't sure if she meant her or a pardre! Anyway it didn't matter. On the way home after smoking all those trendy Gauloise I got a cough on, spat out a phlegm straight into the napkin and she was gone forever. Such is life.

When we got back to Dave's house Jane came down, feeding Johnny and wanting to know how the night had gone. She sat back on the settee, resplendent in her Baby Doll nightie, feeding Johnny: I just didn't know where to look, or how to cross my legs for that matter. Luckily, or unfortunately, depending on how you see it, I was able to hide my embarrassment. Dave was alongside me.

"What do you want for supper," asked Dave.

I'll never know why I said what I said next but the words just tripped off my tongue.

"I'll have whatever young Johnny's having," I replied.

Then I suddenly blacked out. I woke up what only seemed like moments later, but with a throbbing ear the size of a cauliflower which was well in the frame for Vegetable of the Year at the Yorkshire Show. Dave was stuffing a sardine toastie down my throat, a little too vigorously I thought. To a casual onlooker it could have looked as though he was choking me. Dave and Jane carried on as though nothing had happened and the ensuing conversation went something like this:

Jane to me: "How did your night go then? Was the band any good?"

Before I could answer Big Un jumped in.

"The old bugger pulled. He pulled."

Jane to me:

"What was she like? What's her name? Is she short, tall, thin, fat somewhere in the middle, what colour are her eyes, where's she from...?"

I got a hundred questions in one sentence, a talent only women have been able to master.

Rod to Jane:

"Don't listen to him, it was nowt to write home about. She didn't even know the football results."

Jane to Rod:

"What was she like? Was she pretty?"

Before I could answer Big Un jumped in again.

"She was drop dead gorgeous with beautiful golden honey-blond hair and beautiful tanned legs all the way up to her bum."

By now Jane was glaring at Dave. He was getting a bit carried away. Her eyes could have cut him in two but he was riding the wave and wasn't going to stop.

"She had this beautiful smile with just a hint of naughtiness in it, and although she had a beautiful slim waist she had the finest pair of sumptuous breasts any woman could wish for and..." (chucking in a Doddyism for maximum effect), "all full of plumptiousness."

Turning on Dave she finally bit.

"You didn't really notice her then?"

"I had to," he said, "I just couldn't believe the similarities. She was the absolute image of you."

"That's nice," said Jane smiling, deflated

Never believe a Yorkshireman can't be smooth.

Over twenty years later I'd found myself back on the treadmill again. Politicians can tell us that we had a global recession in 2008 but all I can say is they must have kept quiet about this recession during the previous three years. Small companies were dropping like flies as banks were withdrawing their lending facilities. I'd been forced to put my nose back to the grindstone and do several tackle shows. Having done them since the early Eighties I had long before come to the conclusion

I was back on the show circuit to promote the reissue of The Carp Strikes Back. Here I am with John Wilson and friends at Five Lakes.

that they were loss leaders. In effect they involve four days away from your workplace: a day emptying your factory or shop, then most times travelling the length of the country, setting it all up and being on your feet for two days and then (because of the auction-like atmosphere of the weekend) you sell your goods for half their value just to pay the expenses of the weekend.

Young helpers at these weekends love them; out half the night and even enjoying hotel food and facilities like gyms and swimming pools. Me, I get up for breakfast just to make sure I get something to eat before being on my feet all day. Somewhere between 6.00 p.m. and 8.00 p.m. they close. I feel completely knackered and far from the

A Cappella

mood for socialising, preferring room service and 'Match of the Day'. On Sunday you work all day, pack it all down, load it all into the truck then drive home in the dark on chaotic motorways you hardly know and whichever satnav (satellite navigation system) the lead driver has is also not familiar with. The last time I came home from a show the satnav first took us round the Midlands, then did a sharp right then took us for a tour of the Fens! The only reason I did the shows was to bring in some – however little – cash flow during the winter months.

Back to the show in question, which I was actually attending to promote the reissue of my book 'The Carp Strikes Back' by the Little Egret Press. By the time the show had closed on the Saturday I was pooped. It hadn't been an enjoyable day. In the past when I'd attended these events I would see many old friends, but on this day there were hardly any of them there. I had to face it, all my surviving friends were by then in their sixties. They didn't need to buy any tackle because they already had more than enough, on top of which most of them with a free weekend would prefer to go fishing. The event had been well attended but with anglers from different generations to me.

I stopped off in the hotel bar for a couple of pints before heading for the bedroom with the intention of soaking my feet in the bath. So there I was feeling pretty miserable gazing into my Guinness when this very pretty slender girl with long blonde hair who could have been no more than twenty walked up and asked if it was all right if she sat with me. I looked around the room: every other table and chair was empty!

"Yes, certainly," I replied, asking if she would like a drink.

"Yes, I'll have a small white wine please Rod."

She knew my name but as is usual with me I didn't think to ask her hers. It seemed pretty obvious she was working at the show and we went through all the usual small talk about how the show had gone and so on. Somehow the conversation kept going for nearly an hour before I ran dry and asked if she knew the football results, which she didn't. But an hour's conversation between me and a girl was nearly unheard

"Rod, you're useless, you don't even know who I am, do you?"
Dave and Jane's daughter Kit who was working on the Angling
Publications' stand at the Five Lakes show.

of, and I'd quite enjoyed it. I didn't delude myself that a beautiful young lady like her could possibly fancy a creaking old shire horse of a bloke like me: I thought she was just a young career girl hoping for a hand up the ladder of the fishing trade.

I was just thinking of making a move towards my room and the bath when in walked a couple of the young lads who had made a name for themselves in carp fishing.

"All right Rod? How's it going? Mind if we sit with you? And who is this lovely young lady sitting with you?"

I ducked the question. To be honest I hadn't got a clue! The girl turned on me.

"Rod, you're useless. You don't even know who I am, do you?"

I could only shake my head and agree with her.

"Look love you are vaguely familiar. In fact apart from the fact that you're so slim you're the image of a girl I once knew."

I was trying to dig myself out of a hole!

"Rod you don't mean slim: you mean my boobs aren't as big as my mum's. Rod, I'm Katie, Dave and Jane's daughter."

Over twenty years on from that magical moment on the bank at Castle Lake the wheel had turned full circle.

New Adventure, Part One

"Yow, here we go! Eyes down for a full house!" I'm driving a camper van with Annie, the kids, six weeks' bait, plus a boat on the back. Down the ramp and then rev up to make it up the iron slope onto the North Sea Ferry. All the new gear I'd got and the new camper had cost me twice as much as I'd ever spent on a house! But what the hell, you've only got one life.

We were off and away on a six-week summer holiday taking us where we knew not, only that our starting point was Holland and after that taking in some fishing with our friends in Belgium. The crossing was smooth. We hogged the karaoke all night while the kids gambled. Knowing that we would lose an hour's sleep due to the change from English to Continental time I went to bed early, about midnight. Annie and the kids were enjoying themselves and continued partying until the disco closed at 1.00 a.m. English time, 2.00 a.m. Continental. At five in the morning – I forget which version of the time, but I felt like I'd only been asleep ten minutes – there was a knock at the door.

"Your morning tea, sir."

I hate filling in forms but apparently someone had asked for morning tea! I was shattered, but knowing the drive I had ahead I forced myself out of bed and drank two pots of tea while the others snored away around me. Two hours later I was starving and, despite much abuse, managed to rouse the troops. It was hard but challenging Gary to a sausage-eating contest with four rashers of bacon, two eggs, beans and tomatoes brought out the competitive instinct in him. He won with eight sausages, but regretted it for the rest of the day!

Disembarking at Rotterdam we headed north, our first destination being the Twente Canal. Holland may be a small country, and very flat, but our journey took most of the day. It was our first trip out in the brand new camper van, and it was seriously overloaded. Apart from us and the clothes and food we had a full tank of water, 200 kilos of boilies, 100 kilos each of maple peas and maize, plus 50 kilos each of Seafoodblend and Protein Mix in dry mix form in case we ran out of bait. It was little wonder that we never got above 45 miles per hour! Our original aim had been to visit most of the countries in Europe in six weeks but at that speed we would hardly be challenging Phileas Fogg!

Our Dutch host Arnold had a static caravan on its own stretch of the canal at Kristerbord close to the city of Enschede. We had a wonderful time there, with the weather great and everyone enjoying

The stretch of the Twente Canal which was our first port of call in Holland.

the fishing and catching fish. I had a retail shop at the time and had acquired a couple of twelve-metre poles and three-metre whips for the children. In my opinion teaching someone to fish is much easier with a pole. There are no reels to mess about with and none of the frustrating assortment of tangles that occur when people are learning to cast. At its easiest you just tie on a ready-made hooklink and you are ready to go.

The Angling Times front page highlighting Annie's efforts in the 1976 British Pike championships.

Annie with Gertie from Waveney G Lake at 27½lb.

Pausing to enjoy the hops with our old friend Rob Van Den Ing.

I think I should make it clear that Annie didn't need any angling instruction from me! She had been fishing from an early age and had entered the British Pike Championships at the age of twenty, the only female entrant. She didn't win but she did catch and her picture appeared on the front cover of Angling Times. She fished for tench and bream on the Broads and in local ponds, then graduated to carp fishing. At the time we got together her personal best was the famous Gertie from Waveney G Lake at 27½lb. She says that one of her main claims to fame was accidentally baiting up over Kevin Maddocks' baits on 'E' Lake. (Good on yer girl!) For many years she was married to a carp angler but they had been separated for over two years and a half years when we started seeing each other. During our time together Annie wrote a couple of lovely articles for my annual Carpscene magazine-come-catalogue. Back to the story...

At that time the Twente Canal was renowned as a winter carp water due to a number of warm-water outfalls from neighbouring factories: but it was still a fine carp water in summer and most of my pleasure

Teresa and Gary with just a few of the
fish they caught from the Twente Canal.

One of the commons from the Twente Canal.

and match fishing friends would have been thrilled with the quality of the coarse fishing. In three afternoon and early-evening sessions on the pole I caught more bream over five pounds than I had done in my whole previous life. And it wasn't only me; everyone who joined in the fishing caught their share. But I wasn't used to fishing in the close proximity of other anglers. I'd always liked as much space to myself as possible even if it meant walking to the other side of the lake away from where most of the anglers would be congregated. I'd grown up in an era when most of the English rivers were full of fish at a time when the majority of pleasure anglers preferred to fish rivers. On the lakes I fished if there were three anglers on there I'd think it was crowded and very often I'd had lakes to myself.

So picture the scene. There we were fishing Arnold's stretch of canal, maybe 20 yards frontage. On the extreme left I had two carp rods out. On the extreme right Annie also had two carp rods out, and in between we were having a match on the poles. I was in the first peg next to my carp rods. Gary was to the right of me, Teresa to the right of him, Arnold to the right of her, our friend Robert to the right of him, and finally Annie to the right of her carp rods. All this was in 20 yards of bank space and it was pretty tight!

Suddenly one of my carp rods screamed off. I leapt up with a 12-metre pole in my hand and, turning towards my rods, smacked Gary bang on the back of his head, sending him flying into the Twente Canal! The good news was that I managed to land my fish. Meanwhile everyone else managed to rescue Gary from the canal! The problem was that I didn't even know I'd knocked him into the water in the first place, my mind just being set on responding to the run. I was obviously going to need some time to adjust to family fishing!

After a very enjoyable four days we were off with our friend Robert to the south of Holland. There we fished a couple of nights each on

I should have had a good night's sleep instead of spending the night catching small commons on maize!

two of his local lakes, one of them apparently having one bank in Holland and the other in Germany. We caught a couple of carp at each venue we were taken to, but not big ones. The best fish of the trip had been an 18-pounder from the canal, but they were carp all the same. On the final water I had caught my fish from the far margin and Robert insisted that meant I had caught my first German carp.

It was then on to Belgium where we fished one of the country's many canals in the company of our friend Peter. Then onwards again to a gravel pit close to the River Maas where we were to catch our first twenties of the trip. To be honest I would like to have stayed there longer after two fish on the first night. I thought that the water had real potential and that we could have caught a few more, and maybe a biggie, but it was quiet, with little to do for the children. In addition the domestic animals in the area resented the fact that we were on their territory! We were sitting in the camper during the evening when a bull stuck his head through the door! Not long after his herd arrived and they all decided to scratch themselves against the side of the camper before relieving themselves just outside. The following day after a few repairs to the van – nothing major, just new wing mirrors, headlamp and reversing light – we were off through the Ardennes, stopping for a night at a campsite in Luxembourg before making our way into France.

The campsite had a small lake on it and as we managed to park close to the water we thought we might as well put the rods out. In one way I was glad we did, as we caught carp: in another I wish I hadn't fished. Just fishing over a bed of maize with maize hookbaits I had non-stop runs all night long with every fish a common and not one of them above twelve pounds. The following day I was totally cream-crackered with eyeballs down to my knees and had to face a fair drive down into France where we had promised to visit the shop of a good customer that we had in Paris. I felt like a three-day-old take-away with hardly any life in me when we came up to the French border. I think this was in the days before the European Community, and certainly in the days before open borders. At customs we were ordered to pull in, probably due to my appearance and the fact that I had bigger bags under my eyes than the Churchill dog.

They came into the van with guns in their holsters. They say that the hangman's noose concentrates the mind but I can assure you that the sight of those guns did the same for me. Now 25 years ago hardly anyone in France spoke English. I think the only one who did so worked in the British Embassy, and she wasn't very good at it. We were ordered outside while three officials – presumably customs officers – searched the van. Annie went ballistic. She had spent the previous evening washing, ironing and getting the van ready for the journey. It made no difference: everything came out and was thrown here, there and everywhere. Apparently there was a language divide. I tried my best with my limited French but really I was so tired I couldn't be bothered to argue.

They went through everything. All the top cupboards were stocked with flavours. Off came the tops and each one was sniffed by the three of them.

"Parfums des carpes..." I tried to explain as they indulged in the delights of Monster Crab, Chocolate Malt and Shellfish Sense Appeal. My explanation seemed to satisfy them until one opened a bottle of Scopex, then turned to me and said:

"Parfum de whore!"

We were getting through it and thought the ordeal was nearly over when one of them decided to lift up the bed. Underneath were 50 bags of white powder labelled 'The Protein Mix'! One of the officials was quickly on the radio to his office sounding excited, as though they thought they had stumbled across a major drugs shipment. Within minutes two uniformed men came running across the car park attached to sniffer dogs on leads. Now I apologise for any swear words in this book but on seeing the dogs I turned to Annie and said, "We've shit it now!"

The reason for this outburst was that I had studied flavours and the

The Eiffel tower, impressive, but I've worked on scaffolding jobs at greater heights than that!

reactions to them of fish and animals (mainly dogs and pigeons I should add) for close to 25 years. When you make up a bait with Monster Crab in it if there are any dogs in the vicinity you find yourself surrounded by them. These highly-trained sniffer dogs were no different, they just leapt up the steps into the camper and howled! (I knew it was coming! At one time I had a dog called Ben. When I mixed Monster Crab with Shellfish Sense Appeal he just stood behind me howling and barking. I had to give him every tenth boilie I rolled or he'd have had my leg off. Afterwards he'd have a bout of the runs but had the good grace to do it around the base of the roses.)

Well with howling dogs and radios crackling two more officials came running across the car park towards us – this time pushing a wheelbarrow! Soon all the bags of The Protein Mix had been deposited into the wheelbarrow with all the officials following it off into the main customs building for analysis. After about ten minutes I took a walk to the building and peered through the windows. I couldn't see any laboratories, or anything like one, so we went back to sit around outside the van with Annie and the children. All we could do was await events.

It seemed like an hour or more before two of the officials came back with the barrow, returning our bait. I don't know what the exact process of their analysis had been but they both had white powder in their nostrils and on their bottom lips!

We loaded everything back into the van, snarling. As we left one of the officials tapped on the window. I wound it down and he said in perfect English:

"Sorry for the delay sir, have a good vacation."

We drove on into France but it was already early evening. We stopped at a campsite with a lake I had wanted to fish but I was just too tired to make the effort. All the travelling and unloading, then loading up again seven times in two weeks had left me shattered. I needed to hibernate for a few days to recharge the batteries, but life's not like that. In theory I should have slept for ten hours, all night long, but my head was in alarm mode. Although we were parked a good 60 yards from the lake I swear I awoke to every twitch and bleep from the buzzers of the carp anglers around the lake.

I don't know how we did it and have no recollection of the actual journey – only the signposts – but somehow mid afternoon found me trying to cope with the complexities (and perplexities!) of the Paris inner ring road. How it happened, again I don't know, but after going round it twice, still none the wiser, we pulled off, looking for Port de Spain but found ourselves looking up at the Eiffel Tower.

Now the Eiffel Tower is an impressive structure, no doubt about that, but as a long-time scaffolder I was surprised that it isn't much taller than it actually is. In the past I had worked on buildings and structures much taller than the Tower. What immediately came to mind was a job I'd done in South Wales. I'd been contracted to work on the building of a new oil refinery between Neath and Swansea, but the company also put in estimates for other jobs in the area. One Saturday morning we found ourselves on the docks of one of the many shipyards which then abounded in the area. With me were Swansea John and Porthcawl Ernie, who both worked with me as a gang on the oil refinery. The job was to put a working platform around the winch mechanism at the top of a giant crane, built to lift containers off huge container ships.

Now John wasn't the biggest of blokes but he was as strong as an ox and as brave as a bull, but he also liked a drink or two and Friday was his drinking night. On a Saturday morning he wasn't his usual self. We climbed up to the control tower of the crane where the scaffolding had been stored for the once-a-year maintenance job. It was hard work climbing the hand-over-hand upright ladder more than 100 feet high but we all made it, sat down, had a drink and a fag and were soon ready for work. It wasn't a difficult job if you knew what you were doing. Really it was a full weekend's money for a maximum of three hours work.

I was top man (the highest up), John was ten feet below me, with Ernie handing up the gear from ten feet below. I set out all the base for the job and boarded it out so it was ready to work on. Usually John would then leap onto the boards, erect the handrails and take care of everything to do with the safety aspect. But on this day he didn't want to come up onto the platform. I was amazed. Here was a guy who wasn't afraid of anything as far as I was aware. Make no mistake we were high up. The crane tower of over 100 feet rose perpendicular from the side of the concrete pier. I was directly above the water at approximately 170 feet, John below me at about 160 feet above the concrete and mass of iron machinery.

"What's up mate? Aren't you up to it today? A few too many sherbets?" I asked.

"No mate, I just can't get on there! It's nothing to do with the drink. I can't swim!" He said it apologetically, and in his mind it was a suitable explanation but nonetheless I couldn't help thinking:

"Have you ever tried swimming in concrete?"

Having seen the great tower we set off in search of Jean Louis' tackle shop which we had been assured was the haven of all carp fishers in France. How we found it in a city of that size I don't know. I put it all down to Annie who had the homing instinct of a racing pigeon, which is the complete opposite of my mate Mally who would get lost even if he was a lemming. He'd be the one climbing up the cliff while the others were queuing up to chuck themselves over. But somehow we made it, had a pleasant time, some good food to eat, and did a bit of good business, which was nice.

By that time there were four weeks of our holiday remaining. We left Paris the following morning having slept the night in a truckers' park. We'd agreed to meet Jean Louis and his fiancée at St. Cassien in southern France three weeks later.

New Adventure, Part Two

Three weeks to get to St. Cassien from Paris sounds like an absolute doddle, but it isn't if you take the route we took! There were anglers in Brittany who had been writing to us for several years and we'd agreed to go across to see them the next time I was in France. Now Paris to Brittany at 45 mph is a long old hike: you chuck a hard right south of the city and then keep on driving. If you plunge into the Atlantic Ocean you've gone too far.

We started off at Jurgon les Lacs and never had a sniff from the one place we could park the camper. We only stayed two nights, the lake not really being conducive to a family holiday, but in my mind I knew I'd be back after seeing pictures of some of the mighty fish from the venue.

On leaving the small paddock where a local farmer had let us park the camper I got the vehicle stuck as I tried to drive out through the five-bar gate. I couldn't understand it. There was no mud and the grass wasn't even wet, yet the wheels were spinning and the camper was getting nowhere. As I stepped out of the van I happened to look up just before my foot hit the earth. The local electricity supply was primitive to say the least; a single cable dangling from tree to tree! At the very moment that I realised the cable was caught around our roof-rack my foot touched the floor. There was a blue flash and I was thrown some

We christened the water 'The Mere' because it reminded us of Norfolk.

Annie got fed up with all the particle activity and dropped a boilie in the edge to get some sleep. The result was the biggest fish of the trip at 37lb+!

20 feet through the air. Luckily I landed on my head otherwise some real damage could have been done. I don't know if I'd cut off the power supply to the farmer's nearby farmhouse but minutes later the farmer was on the scene. With the aid of a hi-tech long stick with a fork on the end he lifted the cable above the camper roof-rack and away we drove.

We didn't drive far, maybe for an hour or so before we arrived at our next destination. We didn't even know the name of the water. A French angler who lived in the area had told us of a lake where he had seen many carp leaping. He had never fished the water, nor seen anyone else carp fishing there, but he had seen the carp. This really appealed to

We dropped on wall-to-wall carp and
knew that we would be back for more.

me as I love fishing uncharted waters where it's all about potential and the fish have no names. Our presence there was all based on hearsay. The carp could be naïve and ridiculously easy to catch or, as is often the case, the water could be full of big bream which roll frequently.

On the first visit the water level was high, reaching right up to the fences which surrounded the local farmer's fields and reedbeds stretched out for at least twenty yards into the water. It reminded us of the Norfolk Broads and we christened it 'The Mere'.

The track down to the waterside was perilous to say the least. I made Annie and the kids get out of the van and walk as I was scared it might tip over on the rickety old bump-ridden track. Once we were in though it was all peace and paradise – and wall-to-wall carp! When we left after three days on the water we knew we'd be going back. In that short visit we had accounted for fifteen carp, including eight fish over twenty pounds and four over thirty, the biggest weighing just under the 40lb mark. All but the largest fish had been taken on maize.

We headed south and up through the mountains en route to Cassien.

Annie was not only in charge of the catering but
turned out to be an accomplished mechanic, too!

The largest, which fell to Annie, had fallen to a margin-fished boilie. It had been fantastic fishing in a beautiful, tranquil and uncrowded atmosphere.

We were then off to Cassien by the scenic route. On the way we stopped to look at numerous waters, stopping off to fish at just two that took our fancy, namely Lac Paraloupe and the mighty River Lot, sessions at which are both recounted elsewhere in the Carp Along the Way volumes.

Our session on the Lot had been very enjoyable: a real adventure chugging up the river by boat and not seeing another angler, but witnessing a host of wildlife we had never seen before. The journey across country and through the mountains heading for Cassien seemed to take for ever though. The camper broke down twice and the heat was unrelenting. Luckily, just when I was in the depths of despair and thinking that we could be marooned in the wilds forever – this was in the days before mobile phones, remember – unbeknown to me it turned out that we had a mechanic on board, by the name of Annie (and this was years before Kylie in 'Neighbours'). On one occasion Annie stripped the gear box, and then put it all back together and away we steamed! To someone like me who still struggles with the complexities of a tin opener this was nothing short of miraculous.

The last time I had left Cassien had been twenty months previously. Admittedly that had been in December but when we left the water there hadn't been a single angler on there. On my first visit to the lake there hadn't been another angler on there either so this time around it was a bit of a shock to find it being fished wall to wall. True it was August, bang in the middle of the tourist season, but I hadn't expected the scene that we encountered there. Every point, every bay, every junction between one Arm and another was occupied by bivvies. Bivvies? Had they legalised night fishing and not told me about it? When I first fished there night fishing was illegal, which in itself restricted numbers. Either you risked having your gear confiscated, or came off the water each night. Neither alternative was appealing to many would-be

Cassien anglers so in the early days the fishing conditions were self-limiting. Now, within three short years of being discovered by the English anglers, Cassien had become the world's ultimate circuit water, with anglers from every nation fishing it. I couldn't complain. I was one of the anglers who had written about the lake and publicised it, but all the same it was a shock to see how popular it had become.

In truth our session there was a total disaster. We had arrived mid-week and with all the desirable, accessible swims being taken we were confined to Chez Pierre's car park for the first few days until one became available. At least the camper would be safe in there.

Meanwhile we loaded up the old Avon inflatable, a twelve footer we had bought second hand which had formerly been a sea rescue vessel. Little did we realise that the small electric motor we had invested in wasn't powerful enough to drive the boat. On the first chance that came up to get out to a decent swim on the opposite bank we were literally thrown onto the rocks of the first island to the left of Chez Pierre's café. We all survived but the boat was full of water and all the clothes, sleeping bags and fishing equipment were literally soaked. By now the Mistral was blowing at its strongest. We spent two days drying everything out before we dared to venture out in the boat again.

Take two. We were only 50 yards out from the bank when a violent electrical storm erupted and the rain was driven so hard into our faces that it was painful. It was also frightening. The four of us were out in a rubber boat surrounded by carbon rods with thunder and lightning crashing all around us. Once more we were blown onto the rocks, this time close to Gerard's café.

Take three. The wind had dropped and not long after dawn we set off for the opposite bank in thick fog. The problem was that we couldn't see where we were heading and ended up a good 1,000 yards from our intended destination, going through several anglers' lines in the process. That went down well, of course! We were sworn at in seven different languages – simultaneously.

Take four. After finally getting to the point where we wished to

Cassien wasn't at all as I'd remembered if from just 20 months earlier when it had been peaceful and there were no other anglers on the water.

fish, getting the baits and markers out and the two bivvies erected, we dropped off to sleep. On waking up we found a party of anglers setting up ten yards to our left, and another group fifteen yards to our right. Our outside markers were missing, the only remaining one being directly between Annie's and my rod set-ups. Great, we had eight rods out within an eight-yard circle!

Takes five, six, seven and eight I will leave out because you wouldn't believe them. Take nine though was the final straw. The Mistral had picked up again and fires were raging on the hills around the lake. From nowhere a fire broke out on a small hill directly behind us, barely a couple of hundred yards away. Before we knew it the fire was crackling its way through the dry vegetation leading down to the point we were on. I kept thinking it wouldn't reach us, but it did! As fast as we could muster – all of us – whatever possessions and equipment we were able to grab we waded into the water, which was where we stayed until the fire had burnt itself out.

We'd had enough. It was time to get our coats.

We made our way home by the scenic route, checking out the lakes of the French Alps and Switzerland en route. Some looked really tasty and appealing but not once did I get the rods out. After five weeks of constant fishing and travelling I couldn't face unloading the roof-rack again, or blowing up a twelve-foot inflatable by mouth!

The trip back was the full tourist bit starting with a stay on Lake Geneva. It was there that I thought I'd lost my wallet, but hadn't: it had just been cleaned out in a two-day stay, such were the astronomical prices of everything! From there we moved into Germany where we took in the sights of the Rhine Valley. It was all very pleasant and I started to relax. I was even starting to sleep again, and not waking up to the sound of imaginary alarms. But the holiday was over. All I yearned for was home, to see the dogs again and enjoy the sheer luxury of sitting on a decent loo

But already our next trip was being planned. We couldn't wait to go back to The Mere.

Funny Old Year...

It's been a funny old year really. While some good new products have come through not all of my ideas have been met with total enthusiasm. I had what I thought was a gem of a product lined up, namely a PVA bivvy. Think about it: it saves packing up in the morning! However, no one else seemed to go along with the idea. They also said my idea for a mesh bivvy had too many holes in it. Still you can't win them all.

Five or six minutes later she's beaten, but is unfortunately the other side of a dense reed bed.

Now where was I? Yes, it's been a funny old year. It does at last seem that the idea to open some French waters for night fishing is finally working. At first it didn't: in fact I'm pretty sure someone forgot to tell the police of this decision. I paid quite a tidy sum for a night permit, and what happened on the second night? I got nicked for night fishing! Nice one that. Also I forked out for a permit for a boat: within five minutes of putting her in the water the blue van with the flashing light turned up. Yes, you've guessed it: no boats allowed in the area where fishing was permitted! I enjoyed that one, too. You have to laugh don't you?

It was a pretty good trip, that one. I got nicked on the way out for not wearing a seat belt. I should have known the trip was doomed: I've rarely caught anything on the Continent early in the year, and last year was no exception. John Van Eck and I gave it the big 'un, our best shot, for a week for absolutely nothing. We had no runs at all, that is until all the gear except the rods had been packed away ready for the homeward trip. I was just about to wind them in when one roared off. Saved by the bell, so to speak. Well, not really. It fell off at the net! As you can imagine I was not well pleased.

Next trip out was to our syndicate water, Woldview. A cold easterly was blowing and I didn't really expect much. I awoke just after dawn and the grass was stiff and white with frost. The water was absolutely crystal clear, so I was slack-lining. Anyway there I was looking at the cobwebs which had formed in the bow of the line, glistening in the morning sunshine, when suddenly the bow pulled tight, the rod top hooped over and the Baitrunner screamed. With arthritic knees defying medical opinion I was on it like a shot. Five or six minutes later she's

It was a lovely fish, but not Scaley.

beaten, but is unfortunately, the other side of a dense reedbed. With the rod held high I walked down the bank and around the corner of a small bay from where I could pull the fish away from the reeds. Well I could have done if the running lead hadn't been stuck fast in the thick stems. I pulled as hard as I dared, the water erupted and a big scaley flank rolled on the surface.

"Grief," I thought, "I've got Scaley. First fish of the

season and it's a good thirty."

Without thinking I just jumped in, made my way across the shallows to the reeds and lifted her out in my arms. It was a lovely fish, but not Scaley. The clear water must, in some way, have magnified the fish for it turned out to be a double-figure linear. I wasn't disappointed with the fish: in fact I was glad to get one under my belt. I was very disappointed, though, that on a cold, frosty morning I was soaking wet and had nothing else to change into.

Talking about Scaley reminds me of another trip. I arrived one Sunday morning intending to just have a few hours on the float. John 'totally awesome' Dean and Graham 'I'm too good-looking to be a man' Hoffman were just packing up. 'Awesome' had experienced a right result and had about a dozen baits left: he reckoned that I should chuck at least one rod out with one of his baits on because the carp were 'having it'. Fair enough; I didn't want to disappoint my diminutive friend so I lobbed one out into the middle of nowhere so I could concentrate on my float fishing.

In the middle of the day with the sun at its brightest, the temperature soaring and every fish appearing lethargic and disinterested off shoots the nowhere rod! Very nice, thank you, a 24lb common. I wound in the rods and went to the pub for a bit of light refreshment.

Arriving back at the lake later in the afternoon another diminutive friend arrived, namely Eric, then of Eric's Angling Centre. Looking at him I thought of Deany, and then the thought occurred to me that their parents must have been sixties trendies who indulged in the then-fashionable pastime to bonsai the kids. Well we chatted and I told him about Awesome's hit and of my fish and suggested that as I had about six of Deany's baits left it might pay Eric to put one on one rod. This he agreed to do. At nine o'clock next morning I got a phone call at work: it was Eric, and he'd caught a whacking big mirror of 33lb+ on the bait that I had given him, which Deany had given to me. The fish, incidentally, was Scaley, which Graham Hoffman also went on to catch twice, also on that bait. The bait, by the way, was flavoured with

Very nice thank you, a 24lb common on the nowhere rod.

the old Scopex, blended with Rich Strawberry, proving indeed that great baits never lose their effectiveness.

As I left the lake one Saturday I was already making plans for the next session. I didn't want to go home. I'd had a bit of action the night before by way of line bites and fish activity, and one full-blooded run which had resulted in a magnificent leather carp of 28lb 4oz. The lake had fished like a dog for the previous five weeks and I had the feeling that it was about to come alive again. How is it that urgent appointments always occur when the fish are feeding?

Monday morning I rang my mate Mark Lawson who had fished the lake over the weekend, together with 'Stan the Man' and the two Garys from the shop. I couldn't believe it: none of them had had any

A full blooded run resulted in a magnificent leather carp of 28lb 4oz.

action apart from a tiny carp of a couple of pounds to one of the Garys. I was going back that evening so I listened attentively as Mark gave me the full SP. The fish had moved down from the deep end with the sunshine and Sunday had seen large numbers of carp creeping up onto the shallows. The forecast was for light southerlies: the shallows it had to be.

At this point I should explain that this season I seemed to be on one gigantic roll. A carp angler has to have confidence in his bait and the way things have happened to me this year I think I only have to put my bait to a carp and it will take it. When you're in this mood you just know that if you can find the fish you will catch.

We, meaning me, Annie, the children and the dogs – arrived at the lake around 6.00 p.m. It was going to be a race to get set up before dark. Annie and I were sleeping in the bivvy; the children in the camper. I picked a swim from which I could effectively cover all routes into the shallows. The most likely route looked to be through a marshy area on the opposite bank. Should the night cool off there was sufficient water there to hold them during the hours of darkness. Donning waders I made my way through the reeds to the marshy area which I then baited up with about 200 boilies.

Back at the swim all the rods were fitted up with the same terminal tackle that has been doing me proud this season. It consists of tying a loop through the eye of the hook, to which a pop-up is tied tight. A length of rubber tubing about 1" long is then pushed down the line over the eye of the hook, pushing the loop tight to the shank. A size 3 tungsten olivette is then slid down the line and pushed into the open end of the silicon. The end result is a bait which just sits up off the bottom, holding the hook in a perfect position to take hold in the bottom lip.

It was one of those occasions when every cast dropped perfectly. The air was warm, the south wind continuing its gentle lapping past my swim. With the bivvy up I settled back, relaxing while I could because I felt certain that I was in for a hectic time.

At 11.00 p.m. precisely the middle rod rattled off. I hit it and

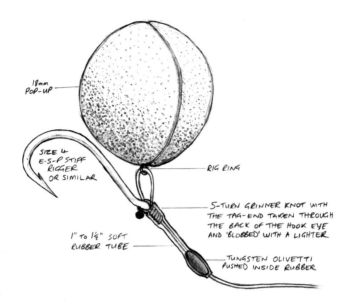

18mm
POP-UP

SIZE 4
E-S-P STIFF
RIGGER
OR SIMILAR

RIG RING

5-TURN GRINNER KNOT WITH
THE TAG-END TAKEN THROUGH
THE BACK OF THE HOOK EYE
AND 'BLOBBED' WITH A LIGHTER

1" TO 1½" SOFT
RUBBER TUBE

TUNGSTEN OLIVETTI
PUSHED INSIDE RUBBER

immediately thought, "Big fish!" Ten minutes later I slipped the net under it. Where it got the energy and power from I don't know: the fish, a mirror, weighed just over 12lb. Small it may have been, but then it was only going to be the first of many... Well so I thought. I awoke at dawn finding it hard to believe that no other runs had come my way. Conditions still seemed perfect; the same warm southerly wind with a cloudy overcast sky forecast. No problem, the fish were obviously going to have it in the day-time. At eight Annie left to take the children to school.

"I'll have one by the time you're back," I said.

Eight hours later and I hadn't even seen a fish, let alone hooked one. Being a quick-thinking sort of fella it occurred to me that there were no fish there! I'd been clueing up shortly before about carp visiting shallow areas. Most of the time it has very little to do with wind direction: it is all down to sunshine. The old sun heats the shallow water very quickly, which attracts the carp. So even in the ideal wind if there's no sunshine there are no carp. There was only one thing for it, I'd have to move. I wasn't sure where the carp would be: the only thing I knew was that

It was a nice chunky mirror carp of 21lb 12oz

they were definitely not in front of me! I decided to move back to the swim where I'd caught the leather from on the Friday. God, how is it that the older we get the larger the heap of tackle and accessories we cart around? I wasn't looking forward to the move round to the other side of the lake at all. It had all the hallmarks of a heart-attack job!

Two hours and five trips later I'd completed the job, fell back and reached for the iron lung. I'd just got the bivvy up in time before the heavens opened. Although no fish were showing I felt confident. On my previous trip I'd learnt quite a lot about the swim. There was still a fair amount of weed about, but I knew the clear areas to my left. Mark had given me bearings in a channel running through the weed to my right. I managed to get the baits out before dark, casting into the clear areas then drawing the line back until the lead pulled up against the weedbed, so positioning the baits tight to the weed. 50 freebies were then catapulted round each bait. The rain had fined down to a light drizzle, while the air remained remarkably warm for mid September. Time to settle back – and eyes down for a full house.

10.00 p.m. and the left-hand rod was away: the sound of the Baitrunner purring in the still night air was music to my ears. The fish went like the clappers, ploughing through weedbeds as though they didn't exist. I kept the pressure on and eventually it tired, rolled and I lifted the net around a nice chunky mirror of 21lb 12oz. Over the next couple of hours I had a number of bleeps on the buzzers without anything really happening. There were certainly fish in my swim but apparently they had still to find the hookbaits.

Around 2.00 a.m. the buzzer to the centre rod bleeped just once. Half a minute later it did it again. I was out of bed and standing by the rod. What the hell was going on? There was a weird vibrating noise: it was the line being stretched against the line clip. For some reason it wouldn't pull free. Instantly I picked up the rod and struck. 40 yards out the water erupted! I'd stuck the hook into something big and it didn't like it. The rod was pulled round faster than I could backwind as the fish surged to my left. I'm sure it would just have kept going had it so wished, but I had a bit of luck there: it ran out of lake! It had only one way to go and that was towards me.

A few minutes later it was in front of the rods. Clambering down the bank in the pitch darkness I slipped on the wet grass. The rod lurched forward, momentarily causing a slack line. In an instant the fish was off. I felt gutted. Not only had I lost a truly big fish and got wet in the process, but it also felt as though I'd broken my back! Oh the delights of carp fishing. I fell back into bed in agony.

Shortly after dawn I was woken by the buzzer to my right-hand rod. I was soon into it, and all the pain was forgotten. After a spirited fight the net folded around a plump 16lb linear. It was a truly gorgeous fish, and one of my babies, the progeny of carp stocked eight years before.

As the daylight grew stronger so did the southerly wind. It felt weird, sitting at the wrong end of the lake, but as it was still very cloudy with occasional light showers I doubted if the fish would follow the wind. Hell I was praying they wouldn't: it was a toss-up as to whether I would survive another move!

The day produced the same amount of action as the day before, precisely zilch! I must have walked the lake ten times without seeing a sign of a fish. I was confident for the night, though, all the hookbaits being in the same positions as the night before. I was ready: all primed up for action. So what happened? Nothing! Not a bleep; not a line bite; nothing. No, I tell a lie. I had a magnificent swan at about two in the morning. I couldn't really count it though because it got off at the net! Dawn came and I scanned the water for fish. There were no signs: no bubbles, no rolling fish, nothing. The lake looked dead. I knew the baits were untouched and exactly where I wanted them to be so I left them out and climbed back into bed.

'Stan the Man' had returned and was now fishing opposite me on the far bank. He'd told me that 8.30 a.m. was the golden time in the swim I was fishing. True enough, half eight came round and my left-hand rod roared off. It was a peculiar scrap. The fish charged off for maybe twenty yards then just stopped and lay doggo on the bottom. I bent the rod for all it was worth but barely managed to budge the fish. Stan yelled across to see if I wanted any help.

"Yes please Stan, I think it's a big one."

I heaved and heaved on the rod, praying the hooklink wouldn't part. Eventually the pressure told and the fish moved off, slowly and grudgingly. I don't know how long it took before it rolled in front of Stan and the waiting net but it seemed a mighty long time. My arms and back were aching and really giving me some gyp.

"It's a mirror," said Stan, "It's the big 'un!"

The fantastic run of luck I'd been having had continued: it was another thirty pounder, my sixth of the season to that point and, at 34lb plus, a true biggy. As Annie clicked away with the cameras I couldn't help but think:

"You jammy sod Hutchinson."

At 10.00 a.m. it was time to pack up and head for work. It had been a session that had pleased me. The fish had not gone crazy but I knew that I had fished well, and that my instincts had eventually put me in the right place.

Moving on, a couple of weeks back I attended a carp show in Germany. Much to my surprise I really enjoyed it and was reacquainted with many anglers whom I had previously met on the banks of waters in Holland and France. The event was much like carp meetings everywhere and it wasn't long before the bar was crowded with anglers swapping stories of the past season, and talking about waters they intended to fish in the coming year.

It's funny but when I meet anglers at dos like that the question I most get asked is "Why do I still fish for carp?"

Well for a start I've never been ambitious. I try to put myself in the right place and after that I'm happy with what comes along. I do still harbour wishes for personal bests – as I think most of us do – and for that reason once or twice a year you will see me on some water capable of achieving those targets. But for the most part I'm happy just to be out in the fresh air in pleasant surroundings simply enjoying the thrill of carp fishing and the company of carp anglers, provided there aren't too many of them on the water at the time. There is without doubt a camaraderie amongst carp anglers, whatever the nationality; a common bond which enables us to join in the crack together.

The variety of rituals I've witnessed when someone has caught a personal best is something else. Some have to throw themselves in the lake: others celebrate with champagne or brandy. At Savay you

The fantastic run of luck I'd been having continued with my sixth thirty of the season, Minty at 34lb+.

were allowed mushrooms with your breakfast. Two anglers from Amsterdam, Burt and Henk, whom Richard Seal and I got to know when we fished the Orient together, even perform a variation of a Turkish belly dance! Not a pretty sight, I can assure you. Let's face it I still fish for carp for the same reason as everyone else does, because I thoroughly enjoy it. Beautiful commons, big scaly mirrors, gleaming leathers and scale-perfect linears: we love them all. So enjoy your carp fishing and I hope you enjoy it for as long as I have done – at the time of compiling this book 47 years, and counting!

More Friends Along the Way

Carting the gear back to the car park I bumped into the Tooth (alias Keith O'Connor, alias Shamus O'Twit) star of stage, screen, video and the Angling Times. Now the old Tooth's had the odd fish or two (including an English 43-12, jammy bathtub) but that isn't what I best remember him for. Tooth and I have holidays together and have generally blown apart Majorca a few times, and I had just received the following postcard from him, straight from Magaluf: "*Dear Rod, Weather awful, beer flat, kids driving me mad, wife drunk every night. Wish you were here.*"

Keith the Tooth, an endless source of amusement, but he could catch 'em, too. Keith with a Colne Valley big 'un from the early Eighties.

Last year the Tooth went round the world. Arriving in Australia after a shattering 24-hour flight he picked up the phone and rang home.

"Hello," said his lad at the other end of the line, "who's that?"

"It's your dad here, ringing from Australia," replied the Tooth.

"Can't talk to you now dad, EastEnders is on," said the boy and put the phone down!

I've got so many stories about the Tooth that sometimes I just look at him and burst out laughing, and this was one such occasion. I couldn't help but think of our last Majorca bash. Six days in and gallons of San Miguel have gone down our throats, plus a few bottles of cheap Spanish champagne, plus a few bottles of local brandy (which doubles for paraffin) and the Tooth hasn't yet been to the toilet! He was as full as the proverbial butcher's dog. Jim Fielding and I thought we knew why. The Tooth is a man of habit: every morning for breakfast, boiled eggs: every dinner, hamburger egg and chips. If he gets a bit peckish in-between meals he eats pickled eggs. In fact if he gets hungry in-between eggs, he has an egg. But now the Tooth is a worried man: even if he could go to the loo he'd be too scared to.

We sit down on the chairs outside an open-air café, the Tooth very carefully indeed. The waiter descends on us, asking for our order. Jim and I go for the old suckling pig. The Tooth's scanning through the menu trying to find something he fancies. He's not used to this. Generally, wherever he goes he just says, "Hamburger, egg and chips," and that's that.

"Come on Tooth, you can't have eggs again, you'll kill yourself," chorus Jim and I. Tooth has that resigned look on his face.

"Yes lads, I know you're right. I think I'll just have an omelette."

Jim and I just looked at each other and never said a word.

I'd been trying to weigh up the bloke who had been standing at the end of our stall all afternoon with two lemonade bottles in his hands. As the day went by his laugh got louder and louder and his nose got redder and redder. Just before I was due to go on stage I got an attack of the jitters. With over a thousand people in the hall it was no time for frayed nerves. I was trying to be responsible and had kept myself sober all day.

The famous Polish renegade Zyg Gregorek, owner of Anglers Paradise.
Zyg did like a drink!

Zyg with one of the fish from his prolific holiday venue.

It was my duty, I thought, to speak clearly and coherently.

"You look nervous, my friend, have a drink," offered the stranger at the end of the stall. "I have a nice drop of wine," he continued, raising one of the lemonade bottles. I was hellishly nervous and a little drop of wine couldn't hurt me, could it? Three glasses later I was legless. He never told me what type of wine it was. Looking back I suspect it was produced from the fruit of a diesel pump.

This was my introduction to the famous Polish renegade Zyg Gregorek. That afternoon his parting words were:

"You must bring the family down to Devon some time and fish my lakes. Maybe we'll drink a glass or two," he added with a twinkle in his eye.

Early the following April we made the trip down for a long weekend. Zyggie was in his front garden when we arrived and immediately suggested a glass to wash away the travelling thirst before showing us to our accommodation for the long weekend.

We were very pleasantly surprised by the quality of the accommodation. Fishermen are generally happy with anything on a par with a second-hand bivvy but Zyggie and his wife Rose had thought hard about the requirements of the anglers' families. If they had everything they needed and were happy, the angler would be too. We were installed in the Wishing Well Lodge, a Scandinavian type chalet. It had the lot, fully fitted kitchen, fridge, bath with piping hot water, colour TV. You name it, it had it, and this wasn't even top of the range.

I was still lying in bed the following morning when Gary came running in: he'd caught a tench, some carp, rudd and a goldfish. Someone else on the same lake had caught over 100 fish. I investigated. It turned out he had been fishing on the Float Lake.

"No one ever blanks on there," Zyggie assured us.

I decided to have a couple of hours with Gary, trying my hand on the roach pole. First drop in and bang, under went the float. In no time at all a gorgeous golden-coloured rudd came to the bank. In two hours we had over fifty fish, all immaculate little creatures: rudd, common carp,

Enjoying some relaxing float fishing at Zyg's.

crucians, koi, golden tench, and even plump little shebunkins. I love catching fish and it was such fun I was reluctant to get out the carp gear.

That night we talked, drank and ate till late in Zyggie's celebrated African bar, which explains why it was gone eleven o'clock the following morning before I made my way across the fields to the main carp lake. I sat for half an hour in one of the front swims without seeing a thing before deciding to take a walk round to see if I could spot anything. Behind the new island I found a couple of fish. Creeping up I dropped a bait on them, then let out line as I walked back to a position out of sight. Maybe ten minutes had passed when the rod pulled round and the Baitrunner screamed. The fish tore round the other side of the island. I ran up the bank towards the fish, not knowing that it would change its mind and swim powerfully back towards me. For a moment it had slack line and the hook dropped out. I wound in and went back for some dinner, letting the swim calm down.

Returning a couple of hours later I positioned a popped up bait on the margin of the island and scattered a few freebies around it. I didn't have long to wait before it roared off. This time there were no accidents and Zyggie arrived as I drew the mesh around a perfectly conditioned common of eleven pounds eight ounces. It was nice to catch a double so quickly but the truth was that I had a yearning to get back to the non-stop action of the Float Lake. After all the hours I spend after carp I find it tremendously relaxing to get the float tackle out now and again.

The following day I tried the Specimen Lake. To cut a long story short I blanked! The fish were there; lovely big-scaled mirrors gliding around the margins as if they hadn't a care in the world, but for the life of me I couldn't get one of them to take a bait. In fairness maybe I'd been a bit lazy. I was still using the tackle from my last foreign trip. It could have been that the size 2 hooks and 15lb hooklinks were a bit crude for them! On our final morning Gary and I had a competition to see who could catch the biggest golden tench. Gary won with a fish of about 2½lb. They are truly beautiful fish, reared by Zyggie himself, and some are well over 5lb.

Albert 'Alf' Romp with Sally the Carp from Savay.
I don't know whether he caught it on my bait or not!

Throughout the summer I kept getting reports on how well the lakes had fished. Numbers of twenties were caught while I think they lost count of the number of doubles that were caught. We thoroughly enjoyed ourselves and hope to go back again. I can't think of any better recommendation. Zyggie tells me that when most of our lakes are crowded out during the early weeks of the season in June and early July his lakes are very often quiet. So if you fancy a quiet start to Zyg's place get in touch with Zyg Gregorek, Anglers Paradise, The Gables, Winsford, Halwill, Beaworthy, Devon EX21 5XT.

I guess we were about a month into the season of 1981, the first year of the Savay syndicate. It was around seven thirty in the evening as I made my way back to the lake after having a pie and pint at the pub. It was a beautiful warm sultry evening with a nice southwesterly breeze blowing into the Cottage Bay, where my pitch was set up. Conditions were as perfect as they could be and, not unnaturally, I felt really confident of a few fish during the night and early morning.

As I passed through the entrance gate two anglers came towards me down the gravel track. One I recognised as Bob Baker (the famous carp angler): the bloke with him I had seen around the water but didn't really know his name, although I had heard him referred to as Alf. As our paths met 'Alf' said, "Coming for a pint, mate?" I explained that I'd just been for one and wanted to get back to my swim. With that Alf went into a long monologue about how nobody liked him, how no one would talk to him, and by the end of this tear-jerking rendition I felt so sorry for him that I agreed to have just one quick pint with them.

That was my intention but somehow I just couldn't get away from him. Every time I tried I got another sob story. Anyway somewhere along the line Alf persuaded me to have a game of pool with him, a game which at that time I had never played before. Somehow or other I won the first game, the second and the third, which was quite remarkable really as by that time I couldn't see the table, let alone the balls! I've always enjoyed a few pints but this night they were getting to me. Unbeknown to me the lager Alf was plying me with was pint after pint of Special Brew – real headbanger gear.

All the time we were playing Alf kept going on about how brilliant I was at pool, a real natural. I should have realised he was up to something when he suggested we play for a fiver, but I didn't. Anyway a fiver got to a tenner, and then up to twenty and I was still winning! I felt sorry for the bloke. I didn't want to take his money, and I'd had no idea that I'd be so brilliant at pool!

"Look," said Alf, "one final game. If you win I'll give you fifty quid! If I win you give me six of your baits."

It sounded a good deal to me: I couldn't lose, could I? It was agreed, the balls were set up, then bang, bang, bang! Alf, who couldn't hit a barn door all night, potted the lot off the break!

Talk about being set up!

I can't remember if my baits did Alf any good or not but what I do remember is, after casting out, bending over to set up my bobbins, the earth started spinning around. I knew I was going to fall head first into the lake and there wasn't a thing I could do about it. Straight through the rods I plunged, snapping them in the process.

In the circumstances it's surprising that I ever spoke to Alf again, but for some reason I couldn't stop myself. He is one of those blokes who just makes you laugh.

One morning he came up to my bivvy and asked, "Are you hungry?"

Hunger didn't come into it, I was starving.

"Come here," he said, leading me towards his swim, "I've got something to show you."

I followed like a starving dog. There, inside his bivvy doorway, on the stove was an enormous frying pan sizzling away. There was the works in that pan: bacon, sausages, steak, mushrooms and lots of other bits and pieces, all cooking to perfection.

"Don't that look great?" said Alf.

"Not half," I replied.

"Yes, I thought you'd enjoy watching me eat it," he said, then proceeded to scoff the bloody lot!

In the wind-up stakes Alf has no equal.

I was late arriving at Savay that Sunday for rota changeover. I'd played football that morning: it had been a cup game and had gone into extra time, hence my late arrival. I thought I would struggle for a decent swim but instead I had the lake to myself! There was a lovely southwesterly blowing down the gravel pit and light waves lapping through The Birches. As I surveyed this beautiful swim a huge mirror topped out. I thought I heard it yell, "Come and have a go if you think you're hard enough."

That was it: my swim had been chosen for me. Before setting everything up I took a rod from my holdall which was already set up and dropped a bait on the fish that I'd seen roll. I then laid the rod on the grass with the clutch set while I set about fixing up the bivvy, bed and all the other paraphernalia we seem to think we need for a two-day session. Finally it was all done and I could settle down, relax and have a cuppa. I was halfway down my first brew of the session when Albert came walking slowly down the path. He was on his own and not looking his usual mischievous self. His bosom buddy Bob 'Bigfoot' Baker was laid up with a bout of gout. Now Albert and Bob together formed a formidable double act with their cutting – sometimes cruel – humour, and they only got away with it because usually it was funny. But on this day, being alone, Albert looked almost vulnerable and was obviously not a happy chappy.

"All right Albert?" I asked. "Want a cup of tea?"

"I'll have a cup of tea but I'm not all right mate. I've had a bad morning."

"What's up Alf," said I, using the affectionate name Albert is sometimes known by. The others are all unprintable. I let Alf pour out his troubles.

"I've been up the hospital all morning with the missus," he said, "and

Wind-up merchant Albert. He had me at it a couple of times
but this time the joke was on him!

things aren't good. She's got to have a kidney transplant."

We fell silent for a moment, Alf being emotional while I felt it was best just to listen. He pulled himself together and continued:

"I asked the consultant what the dangers were and he said possible rejection of the kidney, which could be fatal."

He put his head in his hands for a few moments. What could you say? I let silence prevail. Then, shaking his head from his hands as if in an effort to drag himself from the morose pit he had fallen into, his face suddenly brightened a bit.

"You know I sat there thinking about what the consultant had said and suddenly the answer just came to me. I told the consultant there would be no problem with rejection as long as they made sure it was a male kidney."

"Mr. Romp," replied the consultant consolingly, "all tests prove that male and female kidneys are entirely compatible."

"Look," Alf insisted to the consultant, "just make sure the kidney is from a male and there will be no problem. I've known this lady for twenty years and she's never rejected a male organ yet."

He'd had me on the verge of tears but my eyes quickly dried when I realised that Alf had done me again!

Another morning, as we sat watching some bubblers out from my swim, Andy Little walked by.

"Hey," Alf said, "do you know how he got his name?"

"No," I replied curiously.

"Well, when he was born his mum took one look at him and said, "you may be little, but you'll come in 'andy'".

It is hard to talk about Alf without relating all the strokes that he's pulled and his endless stream of misadventures, but there is another side to him. He is a tremendous carp angler. In all fairness anyone who really wants to can find out about baits and rigs and sort out the technical side of angling. I know Alf, like many others has done this, but I feel this fares little towards his success. He is a natural, as good as anyone I've ever seen at spotting bubblers and leaping fish. The fact that most of them are bream is irrelevant! Seriously, he has that knack of finding carp, the knack of knowing where moving carp will end up. Certainly during the time I fished in his company he made things easy for himself by getting on feeding fish, often fish no one else had spotted.

Alf usually finishes up smiling when he's had me at it yet again!

Ramblings of a Man in Panic

Date-line 10th January 1987: the phone's just rung and the printers are on. They have to have the catalogue in by 1st February. It's been planned for 100 pages. I look down at my desk and looking up at me are 100 sheets of blank paper! I'm in trouble! I read a few of last year's letters: "Marvellous read, smashing articles, lovely photos; keep up the good work." Yeh, easy ain't it? Just pick up the pen and bang out a few articles. It's been easy before, but as the world and his mate's wife knows I've had a bit of a domestic problem this past year and have hardly fished. You have to fish to have the experiences to relate to others. So here I am racking the old brain to remember if anything worthwhile happened on my few trips.

Ah, there were a couple of good hours at Savay when it all came back and I knew the magic was still there. It had been the year of the tiger nuts going into every swim on the lake. Oh they catch fish; they can't help but do so really. Just think about it: unlike other particles or boilies they rarely get picked up by any other species, or break down. I had some in soak once. I'd forgotten about them. On the annual expedition through the garage behind a pile of mouldy boilies I came across this Japanese soldier who didn't know the war was over.

"On yer bike son; the war's over. Get home; you won. People might tell you you didn't, but believe me you did. Go visit London; you'll think you invaded the place."

"Arh, saw," says he.

"Should wipe your bum," say I.

Anyway, where was I? Yes; one year on there's these tigers, with a bit of mould on them, but wash it off and they're as good as new. So what happens on a lake? Chuck 'em in and they're going to stay there until they're picked up. The person in the right swim when they decide to feed is going to catch a few. So if you're on a lake, and the fish are on tigers, then realistically you've got to fish them. But personally, for me that's not enough. I like to think I've done my bit towards the capture of each fish instead of simply being handed what the conveyor belt decides to give me. There's more to fishing than catching fish. Take out the individuality and you take away part of the magic. Catch 'em on your own terms, that's me: a man of principle. If I was going to catch any I was going to get them on boilies. I reckoned, though, that if I had to compete with tigers I'd need a few boilies. A few? I looked like a coalman: two bloody great sacks-full on my back.

Two days in and not a touch: principles are blowing in the wind like leaves on an autumn day.

"Lend us some nuts."

Two days later the rod tops haven't twitched, apart from the odd robin which has stopped by to take the piss.

"Bloody nuts; always said they were useless."

A 15lb Savay common, and I was well pleased to get a notch on my belt.

So it's 'make my way back towards the car park time' and have a final afternoon and night in the bay. I remembered a little gravel bar. I'd often seen fish basking on it during the close season but had never seen anyone carp-fish it. You know, one of those places reckoned to be a noddy swim. It's the middle of the afternoon. I sit down and chuck out a marker float just to make sure the bar is there and is not a figment of my imagination. Sure enough, it's there rising to within a couple of feet of the surface. My confidence has just about gone but I chuck out a couple of pop-ups, bang on top of the bar, just in case the odd browser decides to swim over. No free offerings or anything because really I'm not expecting to catch anything: they're out there on the simple principle that a bait in the water is worth a thousand in the fridge.

Off up the nearest tree for a look around. I'd just got to the top and my buzzer screamed out. No ordinary run this; it's mission control stuff, really giving it the big 'un. Snap, crackle, ouch as I carefully make my way down the tree. With the speed of a bullet – or was it a bucket? – I ran for the rod, deftly negotiating the plank across the swamp. That déjà vu feeling came over me: I'd been there before. Hurtling erratically through the air like a square boilie, sploosh! Oh no: head first into thick stinking mud. Wallow, wallow; slither, slither: I progress towards the rod. The line's still belting out like a good 'un. Pick up in, bend the rod, and crack! Three feet of line hang from the rod top, limp as a spaniel's ear. First run of the season: nice one Rod. Still, it was a run on a boilie, so it was a question of heave the bait in and hope a few fish would creep in that night.

Just before dawn the old birds started up.

"Hello," I thought, "there's the old Optonic bird again. He's really having a go this morning. Hang on a sec though, that is an Optonic!"

Gracefully alighting from the bed, brushing the cobwebs off the brolly ribs with my head and carefully depositing the sleeping bag in the water I was on the rod in a flash. At last, there was one banging away on the end. It kites right at a speed of knots. (Actually I've never seen knots move, let alone speed, but if Crabtree could get away with it so can I!) Oh, deary deary me. The little fellow's got into that thick patch of lilies. I think I'll have to pay it a visit. So in I jumped and made my way to the lilies, winding down all the time.

"Come here sunshine, you ain't going nowhere."

First Savay carp of the season: not as big as usual, a fifteen common, but well pleased to get a notch on the belt. An hour or so later the action repeated itself, right down to the fish getting into the lilies. This time the fish was a bit bigger, a mirror of 18lb 8oz. Life ain't so bad. I lay back on the bed smiling inwardly in quiet contentment as I nodded off. The sun came up, the air became warm, and voices broke the silence as day ticket anglers arrived. Floats plopped in, great balls of groundbait erupted on the surface, and the smell of bacon drifted on the breeze.

Some time later I was into one of those nice dreams where you've a bent rod in your hand and a big fish belting away on the end of your string. It was a great feeling, one of those dreams when you don't want

John Harry, who took some pictures of the 24-pounder, but unfortunately with no film in the camera!

to wake up. Then I realised I wasn't dreaming: it was for real, and the fish really did feel big. No way was this one going to get into the lilies. Into the water again, clutch hard down, don't give it an inch. I'm heaving for all I'm worth. The leader knot slips onto the spool, the fish rolls on the surface and dives into the mesh of the net.

"Got you baby: come to daddy!"

Seemingly from nowhere applause rings out. I look behind me and there are a dozen day-ticket anglers, some clapping. I make my way ashore, handing the net to one of the audience, some laughing, others pointing. It is only then that I realise that I am completely starkers! I look down at the source of their amusement. I look like a white teapot! The scales reveal 24 pounds of lovely mirror carp.

"Cor dad," says a young lad, "that's a monster."

"Not quite, son, mine's bigger than that," replies dad.

Just to complete the morning one of the bailiffs, John 'Know what I mean?' Harry takes some superb pictures for me. It was only later we find out that there was no film in the camera!

I've had one of those gruelling sessions again. Twenty-four hours of nothing. Come to think of it this was my fourth 24-hour nothing in a row. It's been a month now since I saw my last fish. The water has gone crystal clear and I spent a few hours drifting around in the boat. Over three-quarters of the lake's bottom was visible but I still saw nothing. It was obvious therefore that the fish were holed up in the area where the bottom was not visible. Fish there and I'd have them, right?

Wrong. That's where I've fished on my last four sessions. As to why the devils aren't taking the baits I haven't a clue. It's probably something to do with this unnaturally mild weather. I know mild weather is supposed to make fish feed but certainly in the past all my winter catches have come on dropping temperatures. Maybe there is still time yet for a big freeze-up. February is generally the month when it happens. The two days prior to the freeze-up are generally the killer period. Having said that our lake has already frozen over once this winter, back in November.

That was a real turn up for the books and the first time I can ever remember it happening. The weekend before the ice appeared my mate Stan – Stan the Gadgetman – had it off, taking four nice fish. Since the ice melted we've struggled though.

Another puzzler to me has been why I never seem to get a take on the first day. When I was fishing a two-day session all the runs I got came on the second day. Now I'm reduced to a two-day knock not surprisingly the runs have dried up. It's hard to fathom out why a bait has to lie there all that time before it's picked up but that has certainly been the case this winter. Since mid December my usual tactic of a cast every two hours has not paid off at all.

Apart from Stan and me no one else has fished at all this winter, and we fish different days of the week. Consequently with only one angler on the lake at a time it is very difficult to formulate any kind

Struggling on Woldview in winter. Where had the carp disappeared to?

of pattern. Observation from the boat has shown that the carp are in the deep water during the daytime, definitely, and that is where we've concentrated our efforts. However our relative lack of success now has me wondering whether the carp are sneaking up the shallows under the cover of darkness for a feed.

Fishing two swims is the only way I can test this theory out but for the life of me I don't think I can handle carting around the mountain of gear needed for winter fishing twice in a day! It might be successful but it would be bloody hard work and I don't think fishing should be that. It should be enjoyable, not an endurance test. Chances are I'll probably stick in one spot and watch the vast array of birds go about their business. Several migrant birds who were supposed to stop off for a breather have found the mild weather to their liking and have taken their vacation on our lake: the way some of them are behaving I wouldn't be surprised if they took up residence.

Meanwhile it's back to the motionless indicators and my one-sided conversations with the dogs.

"What do you call a deer with no eyes?"

"No idea."

"Correct. What do you call a deer with no eyes and no legs."

"Still no idea."

"Correct."

Come on you lot, laugh; it must be the way I tell 'em!

On another subject, I have just got to drop in this little snippet, because it made me smile. Close to Woldview is a small town that shall remain nameless, mainly because I'm not quite sure if what I am about to describe is entirely legal. In small towns, shops try to be everything to everybody: they have to diversify in order to survive. So, there I was, stocking up with tobacco and chocolate bars prior to a session in this delightful little shop which served as a tobacconist, sweet shop, tackle shop, and hairdressers, all in one. As the lady behind the counter was totting up my few items, the proprietor was finishing off a client's haircut.

Brushing him off, the proprietor said, "Anything for the weekend, sir?"

"Yes please," came the reply, "I'll have two pints of pinkies and a pint of casters."

I had to chuckle.

Crazy Carp of St. Genez D'Olt

"If you want to catch carp you must go to St. Genez," said the French gentleman in his broken English. "There you can expect four or five, maybe six, fish in a day."

That was the kind of action I was looking for; somewhere where all the family could have some sport. St. Genez D'Olt is really a river which has been dammed and for ten kilometres opens out into a very beautiful tree-lined lake. Six years ago it was drained and many fish were lost. However in some of the pools which remained specimen carp to over 40lb were present. While the lake was being refilled the carp bred at a fantastic rate in the relatively shallow water. Today the lake has depths down to 80 feet or more in places and there are carp everywhere.

When we visited the lake temperatures were hovering around 110°F and for that reason we chose to fish where a small river entered the lake: we figured that this might provide a supply of oxygen which the carp would appreciate in the hot temperatures. Our swim sloped off gradually from four feet in the edge to 45 feet 60 yards out. I set our markers at 20 feet and baited heavily around them, one with sweetcorn the other with maize. Both particles had been soaked in a solution of Aquamino.

100°F and still they fed!

Annie and Gary with a morning's catch.

Crazy Carp of St. Genez D'Olt

Around half eight in the morning the action started when one of the sweetcorn baits was picked up. The fish tore around making several runs of 30 yards or more and took getting on for ten minutes to land. I was amazed to find that it only weighed eight pounds! By 12.30 I'd had enough sport for one day: in four hours 22 carp had been landed! All had fought with the same intensity as the first one. They had simply never been hooked before in their lives. Some took up to 15 minutes to land, yet none weighed more than 11lb!

That first day the fish we caught came from by the marker baited with sweetcorn. The second day the peanut swim came alive while the sweetcorn bed produced only occasional runs. By lunchtime 18 fish had been landed, of a slightly higher average weight than the first day when all the carp were commons. The peanuts produced lots of beautifully marked mirrors. Our tactics were simple by today's standards, either three grains of corn or a single large peanut fished on a short Hair on a size four hook with a six-inch hooklength, the lead being semi-fixed. Such action is hard to find so I took the opportunity of trying a great variety of hook patterns. It was for this reason that many fish were lost. Although we landed 42 fish during our first two mornings another 22 had been lost, most of these on a hook pattern similar to that used by long line fishermen. Now while I accept that once fish are hooked on this pattern it is very difficult for them to get off, they can be exceptionally difficult to get a good hookhold with at the outset. In my opinion carp enthusiasts are better sticking to tried and tested patterns.

Day three started in a blaze of action with young Gary having runs on three rods at once! This time the baits were peanut/sweetcorn cocktails. Annie and I were on hand to help him and all three of them were landed, two of them being doubles. We had to retire from the bank early that day: by noon the temperature had risen above 120°F, although while it was too hot for us the carp just continued feeding! During the afternoon we were visited by a French journalist who asked if he could come the following day to take pictures and do an interview.

Yours truly with a lovely linear.

He was emphatic that we use boilies so that he could see the 'English methods'. For my own part I'm not bothered what we catch them on as long as we catch them, but we agreed to his request.

Generally when carp haven't seen boilies before I like to prebait but as this was out of the question we used an ethyl alcohol flavoured bait, Juicy Fruit, which disperses from a boilie much quicker than standard flavours.

The following day you would have thought that we were in the north of Scotland. It was pouring with rain and very cold indeed and it came as no surprise to me that after two hours we still hadn't had a run. I reeled in one rod, replacing my boilie with what I refer to as The Cheating Rig. This rig is one I have used several times on the Continent when I'm not quite sure which bait the carp will prefer. It is simply a hookbait consisting of a single grain of corn, a large peanut and a boilie. It gives you three chances in one.

The bait had been out about twenty minutes when the rod top

whipped over and the beautiful sound of the Baitrunner clutch purred smoothly away. The moment I bent the Sabre 13-foot rod into the fish I knew it was bigger than the fish we had already been catching from the water. There were cameras clicking away everywhere as Henri our French journalist friend did the honours with the net. The fish, though not massive by French standards, was in superb condition, a true linear reminiscent of many Redmire fish I'd caught in the past. It weighed a shade under 21lb.

Gary was the next to have action hitting into a big common which we estimated at around 25lb and was desperately unlucky when the hook pulled on the point of netting. Although no more big fish came our way that day at times the action was incredible. In all we netted 26 fish, many of them doubles, to take our tally for four days to 80 carp.

One interesting point was that the first day we sacked the first dozen fish or so for fear of scaring off the shoal if we released them immediately. However after running out of sacks we were forced to release the fish into the swim straightaway. Much to our surprise this made no difference to our catch rate so from then on we returned the fish as we unhooked them.

There are undoubtedly really large carp in St. Genez, and I wonder how we would have fared if we had used boilies from the outset. I think it was more than coincidence that the better fish fell to boilies. St. Genez lies amongst some of the most beautiful scenery in the whole of France and whilst a boat is essential to see the whole of the lake there are many areas where it can be accessed from the road. At the time of writing it is uncrowded and unspoilt and for sheer action it is a carp angler's paradise.

Sessions on Woldview

As usual Woldview, my syndicate water, opened on 1st April. A working party had also been set for that date, generally just to tidy up the swims and let the new syndicate members meet the existing ones. Although it was overcast the weather was mild and despite a certain amount of suspended algae colouring the water things looked promising with the prospect of a good season ahead. It came as something of a surprise, therefore, when five weeks into the season not a single fish had been caught, and this despite the fact that more rod hours had been put in during this period than ever before in the lake's history.

With the newer members this was probably understandable. By all accounts far too much bait was going in at a time when fish are traditionally slow to move, and only feed spasmodically. But I would have expected those who knew the water to have ticked a few over. Some were getting worried. "Had something happened to the water?" they were asking. Although in my mind I had no reservations on that score there was no disguising the fact that things were slow, to put it mildly! It was time for me to get the rods out for a bit of reassurance.

When you are involved in the tackle and bait trade May is the busiest period on your calendar and a 24-hour session was the most I could fit in. Arriving on the Friday evening I was surprised to find that I had the lake to myself. Conditions were not good. There was a slate grey sky and a chilling easterly wind that blew foam-crested waves into the west bank. First session out I had no desire to be chilled to the bone so I set up on the east bank with the wind behind me at a point where I could, if I wished, fish a on a long line into both deep and shallow water. I didn't see a fish that evening, but I was still confident. Some of my best catches have come when the fish haven't been showing themselves.

Fifteen hours later I was having reason to doubt that confidence. I'd not had a sniff. I'd still not seen a fish either, although in all fairness a fish would have had to fling itself clear of the water to be seen as the wind and suspended algae made fish spotting very difficult indeed.

Around lunch time Steve Brown arrived and set up to my left in the deeper water. Although I'd visited the shallows every hour or so that morning without seeing a sign of fish something told me to spend my last few hours there. I've always found fish easier to catch when they are in shallow water, the main reason being that I'm convinced the only reason they are there in the first place is to feed. That is not to say they don't feed in deeper water, just that there are many periods when they prefer the depths because they are more comfortable there. Because they are cold-blooded carp behave in harmony with their environment. If it's cold they can't switch the central heating on or put on an extra jumper. If it's hot they can't take a cold drink or switch a fan on to get more air. Instead, whatever the conditions are at any given time they find the areas where they are most comfortable. But those areas are not necessarily the best feeding areas. At times of low food intake there may well be sufficient food close at hand. At other times when there is a need for a substantial food intake hunger takes over from comfort and those areas with the most accessible or abundant food supplies – which, more times than not are the shallower areas – will be visited.

Shallows to me mean food; food means feeding, and feeding fish are the easiest to catch. My hunch paid off. Only minutes before I was due to pack up my left-hand bait positioned between two islands, was picked up. All went well until the final few moments when I drew a nicely-scaled upper double towards the net. On seeing the cord the fish found a last reserve of energy and dived deep. Unfortunately the lead didn't follow it as it had snagged in the mesh and the hooklink broke just above the hook. It was unfortunate, but I wasn't too downcast. At least I'd proved to myself that there were fish moving, and that they would take bait.

The following weekend Lee Jackson came up north to do a slideshow for the local branch of The Carp Society, accompanied by Richard from the Tackle Box at Sutton at Hone in Kent. While they were up here I arranged for them to have a night on the lake with my Dutch friends John Van Eck and Alex Van Der Geer. Some fish had at last started to move with Lee and John both taking fish a few ounces short of twenty pounds. The interesting thing to me was that both fish had fallen to the same bait, RH1 Essential oil. It wasn't really surprising that John had used the oil as he and Alex caught a stack of fish on it whilst doing the original fieldtesting for the product. Lee had been persuaded to go for it on the strength of the results of Tackle Box customers using the oil during close season sorties to Devon and Cornwall.

Not being slow on the uptake I planned for a session the following weekend, and during the week made a couple of batches of bait based on the oil, using it in both the Essential Oil Mix and the Red Seed Mix.

31lb! What a start to the season:
Hutchy's luck prevails again.

As it always does when you are really looking forward to a session the
week dragged by, but eventually the weekend came round and Friday
tea time saw me pulling into the car park at the top of the lake. I knew
that later that evening the Hereford lads Shamus, Arthur and Jason
would be arriving so it was very much a case of picking a swim for the
whole weekend as movement was bound to be limited once the lads
had settled in. The previous weekend the fish Lee and John had caught
had both come from deeper water close to the dam wall. However the

weather forecast had predicted moderate southwesterly winds coming in during the Saturday, with plenty of sunshine. Now if anything was going to get the fish onto the shallows those conditions were, although looking at the lake that Friday evening with a northeasterly blowing up to the deep water and drizzle in the air it was hard to imagine that conditions were going to change so dramatically in the next 24 hours. I made my choice: the shallows it was going to be. I just prayed that the weatherman had got it right!

The Hereford lads arrived a couple of hours later and couldn't believe their luck that the swims at the opposite end of the lake with the wind blowing into them weren't taken. Meanwhile the shallows in front of me were utterly devoid of fish, just as I would have expected in those conditions. All I could really hope for was a good night's sleep.

I was woken at dawn by an Optonic sounding and a Baitrunner purring its heart out. Yippee, a run! I fell out of the bivvy, still in the sleeping bag, put my hand over the clutch and struck. The rod arched over and all I could hear was, "Quack, quack, quack!" A bloody tufty had torn me from Annie's side. No point getting upset about it. After all I'd had a run that had set the adrenalin going. Deep down I was starting to worry. The dawn was quite cold and the wind was still blowing from the north. I went back to bed with my fingers crossed.

The morning passed uneventfully, apart from the wind gently subsiding. The lads came round for a chat and reported that all had been just as quiet at the deep-water end of the lake.

Some time around one in the afternoon the clouds starting breaking up and the glorious sun shone through them. Within no time at all the air really started to warm up and we had the first true day of summer. On went the T-shirts and it was sun-bathing weather. My hopes rose with the sun and moments later they positively soared as a gentle ripple came lapping into the bank at my feet. I sat there thinking that if the fish weren't there already they soon would be otherwise my name was Engelbert Humperdinck. For about an hour I sat behind the rods, humming "Please release me, let me go...", and expecting one to go at any moment – willing one to go.

I decided it was the wrong thing to do, for a watched pot surely never boils. I moved away from the rods, switched my mind off, and nodded off in the warm sunshine. I don't remember hearing it but I'm sure the buzzer must have sounded because one moment I was asleep, the next moment I had the rod in my hand with a powerful fish belting away on the end of a tight line. From the other end of the lake the lads saw that I was in and came running down the bank. I'm not quite sure if it was the power of the fish or me being rusty from lack of fishing but it seemed an age before the carp was beaten and ready for the net. I was in a daze. I can't even remember who netted it for me, but whoever it was made no mistake.

On opening the mesh I recognised the fish as one which I had caught a year earlier at 29lb. As is usual on early-season sessions I forget some item of tackle, and on this occasion it was the scales! Jason quickly shot round to his swim, returning with the big Salters. Round the needle went: 29, 30, 31lb! Yippee. What a start to the season; Hutchy's luck prevails again!

I was still as high as a kite when it was time for tea in the camper. I don't think it would have mattered if I'd not cast out again but conditions were now perfect for the swim I'd chosen. On top of that there is one spot in the shallows which, when the fish are there, can generally guarantee a take at a certain time of day. It was too good an opportunity to miss so I rebaited and cast to 'the six o'clock spot'. After the long winter the fish must have been a bit disorientated because the take came half an hour late! Still, better late than never, and well worth waiting for as it was my first common of the season, 21lb to be precise.

Before the session was over I was to see another cracking fish on the bank, this time a new lake record common. On this occasion the fish didn't come to my rods, but those of Shamus Hayes. At 25lb 8oz it made Shamus's long journey from Hereford truly worthwhile, and what a start to his first year in the syndicate!

In the next month I was only able to find the time for one afternoon

Shamus Hayes with his lake record common of 25lb 8oz.

and evening session, but it was a few hours of special interest to me. I'd gone up to the lake with the express intention of stalking fish on particles. I'd chosen to fish peanuts simply because I didn't think they had been used on the lake for quite a few years, during which time a great many fish had been bred and grown up in the water and because peanuts, when new – which they would be to the new fish – are a brilliant bait. Conditions were again ideal, with a warm southwesterly blowing into the islands and light cloud just masking the sun. It wasn't long before I found a group of fish moving up and down the marginal shelf leading into the shallows.

It was fairly easy to predict which way they would be heading, and it was easy enough to lay down a carpet of bait ahead of them. Soon I was sitting back behind the bulrushes waiting for them to come across the baits. Maybe ten minutes had passed before the first tell-tale bubbles rose to the surface. Moments later the lobe of a tail peeped out, quickly followed by another. Standing up and peering over the rushes I was heartened to see eight fish in all, up-ending and feeding ravenously on the nuts. Expecting a run at any second I glued my eyes on the rod tips, which were pointing slightly skywards. As I watched the left-hand tip dipped over. I expected the line to pull from the clip but instead the tip whipped back. Minutes later the right-hand rod went through exactly the same procedure, and even before the exercise had been completed the middle rod was doing exactly the same thing! Three takes, but not a single run, and this when the fish were feeding hard. I wound in each rod in turn. On all three the nut hookbait had come off the Hair. After first firing out a couple more pouches of nuts ten yards further up the bank I recast to this new area, hoping that once the carp had finished the carpet of bait they were then devouring they would move down the shelf and find the newly baited patch.

My luck was in and half an hour later they were on the new baits. This time I stood up behind the rushes and watched them. Into the swim they came, heads moving from side to side taking a nut, first from the right, then from the left. The rod tip dipped as the fish moved its head to the left to pick up another bait, the nut snapped off the Hair and the tip sprang back. The best of it was that I was sure that avoiding the hook had been done unconsciously and not deliberately. The nuts were being swallowed one at a time, and the carp were first taking in a mouthful before they crunched them up. The fact that I was using a fixed lead and tight line either pulled the nut from the mouth of the carp, or snapped the Hair.

I thought back to the big bags of fish my mates and I used to take in the Seventies. Surely the fish fed in just the same way then, yet the methods we used regularly caught bags of fish, not just odd ones. It was 'all our yesterdays' time! Off came the big 3oz lead and on went a ¾oz one on a link swivel with no stop knot, so it was completely free running. Off came the Hair and a single nut was lightly hooked onto the bend of the hook. After over-casting the feeding spot I gently drew the bait back among the feeding fish. After first slackening off the line I placed a light indicator of silver foil between the reel and the butt ring. No more than five minutes had passed before the foil glided up to the ring. A coil of line tripped off the spool and up the foil glided again. The nut had been taken and the carp wasn't even aware anything was wrong. It realised it had a problem when I put the pickup in: it went crazy!

To cut a long story short I had one of the most enjoyable evening's fishing I'd had in a long time, finishing the session with three nice doubles. I've thought about it a lot since then and have come to the conclusion that for fishing close-in particle fishing the original methods are far superior to modern day tight-line, heavy-lead tactics. They are fine for long-range work and boilie fishing but when it comes to particles in future I'll be using the old methods. If you think back, like I did, how many of you have enjoyed more successful particle fishing with big leads and tight lines than you did link-legering? For years I put inferior catches down to angling pressure; now I think that assumption was wrong; I think it was down to bad application of a method, one fine in another context, but not in this one. My mind's made up on this one: I suggest you try it for yourself.

Two weeks after that session I was back again to fish the afternoon and evening. Conditions were superb – identical to the day when I'd caught the '31' – with a warm wind again blowing into the shallows. This time I set up on the west bank of the shallows, electing to fish particles with two rods with Seed Bait Sense Appeal on the other, this bait being popped up two inches off the bottom and attached by the

Woldview at sunset

From the moment I hit it I just knew there was a big fish on.

loop eye rig. There were plenty of fish about and in the first hour I took fish of 14lb and 18lb on peanuts. More fish looked to be on the cards until the mallards came in and went potty on the nuts.

I was quietly cursing to myself when the right-hand boilie-baited rod was away. From the moment I hit it I just knew that a big fish was on. The fish absolutely tore off, straight up the lake out of the shallows and into deeper water, where it slowly bored around, hugging the bottom. Once it was out of the shallows it was away from all the snags and potential danger so I just took things easy and let it slowly tire itself against the bend of the rod. I was in no hurry and consequently a full thirty minutes elapsed before I got my first glimpse of the fish. It looked massive, in the mid thirties, and although I didn't recognise the

CARP ALONG THE WAY

It turned out to be the first fish
of the season, now at 34lb+!

fish I imagined it would have to be Minty, one of, if not the biggest fish in the lake. It was not until a further fifteen minutes had passed though before I was able to make a positive identification within the folds of the landing net. I wasn't far wrong on the weight at 34lb 8oz but the fish was a complete surprise. No wonder I'd not recognised the fish: it was the same one I'd caught at 31lb only weeks earlier. I'd never have imagined in a million years that the fish could put on 3½lb in that space of time. It was obvious the largest fish in the lake were coming up to spawning time.

Later that afternoon I had the chance to catch one or more of the real whoppers when I found five fish all tight together further up the margin. The smallest of these was a common I put at around 28lb, the largest two being Scaley which I estimated to be at a minimum weight of 36lb and Minty which looked close to 40lb. Why I didn't just lower a bait to them and lie back out of sight I don't know. Instead I threw out a couple of handfuls of peanuts just in front of them. Unfortunately they landed too close and spooked the shoal, blowing my chance. I waited for a couple of hours in the hope they might return but it didn't happen. It was daft. I was so disappointed with blowing my chance that I forgot I'd had a terrific afternoon catching three fish, including a real whacker. The fact was I'd blown my chance by taking too much for granted and not showing those lovely big fish enough respect by being careful in my approach. I think the capture of the earlier fish had made it all seem too easy.

Pressure of work meant I only managed two more sessions before winter set in, the first of these being a short five-hour session during the first week in August. When I arrived at noon I found half a dozen fish milling around in and out of the deep corner of the east bank. I'd spent close to an hour trying to get them interested in floaters but all to no avail when a fish crashed out fifty yards to my left further up the deep bank. I just had to go and investigate. I'd just got level with the spot where the fish had shown when the buzzer sounded on my unattended rod. I gave it my best shot and put the old legs into overdrive but by the time I reached the rod the fish had made 100 yards down the bank and gone round a willow I'd planted on a shallow bar. I even saw the fish before the hooklink broke on a steel scaffold pole securing the tree. If I said what it was it would only sound like another 'one that got away' tale so I'll just say that whatever its size I'd love to have landed it.

About half two I moved down onto the shallows with the intention of fishing sprouting chick peas on a known bloodworm bed in the shadow of a dead tree which had fallen over in the shallow water. As I approached the bottom bank a small carp, no more than about eight pounds, flipped over close in on the end of a rush bed. After what had just happened at the opposite end of the lake I was in dire need of a bend in the rod and a fish on the bank. With one rod still having a boilie on I quickly flicked it out to the end of the rushes before walking round to the opposite bank from where I could more easily bait around the dead tree with particles. This took no more than three or four minutes, during which time the rod I'd cast out was always within my sight.

Returning to the swim I was surprised to find my KJB rod pod upside down in the water. I was still trying to work that out when it dawned on me that the rod I'd cast out was missing! To this day it still is. Maybe I'd left the pick-up on and the Baitrunner off, which wasn't really an oversight: I just didn't expect things to happen so quickly! One thing I can tell you is that if you use big 4500 Seaspin Baitrunners like I do don't expect your rods to float. I spent a good hour wading round trying to find the missing rod but had no luck at all.

I sat back on the bank scratching my head but then my eyes lit up as first one fish, then another, began rolling in the coloured water created by my wading. I'd witnessed a similar event at Redmire nearly twenty years earlier and spoken about it in books and at slide shows. There is no doubt at all that carp are attracted to coloured water and on that score raking a swim would just have to attract carp. It was one of those avenues I've meant to pursue some time but never got around to yet here again was more irrefutable evidence of its effectiveness. I'm absolutely sure it was the coloured water which got the fish on the feed.

Each fish I caught had bred in the lake. A nicely-sealed mirror of 18½lb and a common of 20¼lb.

Inadvertent it may have been but it lead to another three fish on the bank in the next couple of hours, all falling to sprouting chick peas and link-leger tactics. The really rewarding aspect of the occurrence was that each fish I caught was one which had been bred in the lake. Two were mirrors with lovely heavy scaling weighing up to 18½lb and the other was a scale-perfect common of 20¼lb.

My last session of 1990 on Woldview came during early September. This is a terrific time of year on the water and in decent conditions you can almost predict where the fish will be at any given time of the day. That is not to say you will necessarily catch them at any given time of the day, but if it's possible to get in the right place – other anglers permitting – you can be in with a very real chance around the clock. On the other hand if there are a few anglers on the lake you can bet your life each will get a chance or two at the time when the fish move close to their swim. On this occasion both days saw three anglers on the water and each had their chances.

In some respects knowing the water well can be a bit of a disadvantage to the morale. I knew with an hour or so when I'd be likely to get a take, but I also knew that the chances where I was were slight for nigh-on 24 hours of the day. It may sound daft to some but the night swim had gone, and so had the dawn swim. I couldn't moan as I had the 8.30 a.m. to 10.00 a.m. swim, which meant that a good night's kip was assured. True to form Richard in the night swim took two nice fish to just over twenty pounds. The dawn swim produced two chances with an 18-pounder being landed, while I had three chances, landing two of them, both commons weighing in at 19lb 12oz and 20lb 2oz. I did try other spots throughout the day but not with any confidence, doubting the fish were even present. If they were they weren't inclined to feed.

But it was a nice session all the same coming at my favourite time of year. It was meant to be just the first of many I would be spending there throughout the autumn and early winter but little was I to know that it was the last time I would wet a line there in 1990. Business had to be taken care of. All my Woldview sessions together added up to less than 200 hours fishing, which is probably why I can remember every moment. Although in terms of hours it may not seem much having less time than I usually do and being more focused I feel I learnt more this year than I have done for quite a few seasons, lessons which I'm sure will help me no end on future seasons.

Still Smelling The Roses

For two solid days it went on, precisely nothing! I had to be losing it. I just couldn't believe we were getting no action whatsoever. Every hour or so the wind would spring up, and with it my spirits would rise: fish would start leaping: I'd be all primed up ready to leap for the rods, then just as suddenly the wind would drop and I knew it wouldn't happen.

This routine had gone on throughout the session. All the time the buzzers sulked, having lost their voices, while rigor mortis had set in on the bobbins. I couldn't settle, being up and down like a blue-arsed fly. I was kidding myself constantly. Every hour I'd convince myself that we were just coming up to the hot time, but each time the hot time was either too hot or too bloody cold. God, things were getting that bad I was even thinking of reading one of Tim Paisley's books. He has more blanks than most: he'd know how to handle it for sure.

In the end I did what everyone else does eventually: I cracked! Years before Lenny Middleton had told me that when you've tried everything you know, but nothing will work, that is the time you have to pay the lake. The price was a ten pence piece, not a penny more, not a penny less. Pay the lake, that and say the magic words and everything would work out OK.

Scrounging ten pence off Annie I made my way to the water's edge, tossing the coin high out over the tight-fisted lake, I said out loud:

"Come on lake, I've paid my dues, be good to me."

I turned my back on the water and walked back to Annie. Suddenly a buzzer shrieked. I spun round, not believing my ears. It was true enough; Annie was into a flier!

"That's not supposed to happen," I thought. "I must stop wearing these tight pants."

Meanwhile Annie was on the end of a bent rod engaged in a battle with one pretty irate carp. Duly landed it was a beauty of 28lb, a fish I would have dearly loved to catch.

We discussed the situation. Could we pull off the trick in reverse? Off to the water's edge walked Annie. The coin was tossed high in the air and the immortal words were uttered. I perched on the edge of the chair, coiled like a spring and ready for action. Two years later I'm still waiting!

Another time, another place. Mark Lawson was fishing with us. It had been a funny sort of day. We were on a hungry water and during the morning I caught a couple of fish, including one which Mark had caught the day before. During the afternoon Mark caught a mirror which turned out to be the other fish I had caught that morning! Just before dark Gary caught a lovely heavily-scaled mirror of just over twenty pounds. A couple of hours later I struck into a belting run, which I eventually landed.

We were by this time a little the worse for wear as the vino had flowed, but there was no doubt in our minds though that what I had caught was Gary's fish again! Mark did the netting and amongst the confusion of tangled lines we shone the torch on the fish. There was no doubt about it; it was Gary's fish again. Mark nodded in agreement before walking back to his bivvy. A minute or so later he was back.

"You know that fish of Gary's?" he said, to which I replied:

"I should do, I've seen it three times in the last couple of hours!"

"Well it's in the sack, as is the other one you caught!"

We looked at each other and burst into laughter. What a pair of plonkers! The moral to this story is that when the Bordeaux flows things aren't always what they appear to be.

Meanwhile don't ever imagine that all foreign trips are romantic, easy times. Take the five days Annie and I managed in the Canaries: well four really because the first was taken up waiting for a jeep that never arrived, then hiring another, then finding out that the few anglers who had been before us had emptied every supermarket within two hours of the lake of sweetcorn. Nice stroke that one. The worst thing was that the supermarkets all told us to go back on Thursday, and we had to be packed up and gone by Friday! That meant we would have just one afternoon and one night when we would have enough bait for a hit.

As it was I'd taken out 20lb of hard maize in my gear as a standby, but maize never has been, and never will be, as instant a bait as sweetcorn. Maize is a great bait but one which needs prebaiting in just one spot for it to really do the business and I for one on such a short holiday could not sit in one swim waiting. We also had one bag of boilies with us, which Annie insisted we take despite my conviction that they'd be a waste of time.

"You just never know," she'd said, "it might just be the big ones that will pick up the first boilies."

The flavour was totally irrelevant as the carp had not seen boilies before. If one was to be taken it would only be because a carp had decided to see if one of those hard round things was edible. I had taken the precaution of dying the boilies yellow, though, just on the off-chance that some half-blind carp might mistake one for a chunk of corn. Not that I intended using them anyway; it was just Annie who insisted on fishing a boilie on one rod.

To some the drive up to the lake would seem pretty uneventful, despite the fact that I had to change my shorts three times. Nearly getting wiped out by other cars is probably run-of-the-mill for these yuppie types belting round in the Porsches, telephone in one hand and steering wheel in the other, whipping from one lane to another on the southern road circuit, so our journey hardly merits a mention...

When we eventually made it to the lake – what a shock! It was the colour of lumpy gravy, due to a rise in water levels of about five feet during the previous week, so the locals informed us. Still we were there, so we gave it our best shot.

A swim on the opposite side of the water entailing a two-hour assault upon a rock face and a team of Sherpas to get the gear round had been recommended. What the hell, I thought. I bunged a couple of fresh Duracells in the pacemaker and went for it. What a bind that swim was. I don't mind blanking but getting eaten alive by ants does tend to piss me off!

Another source had recommended a swim by the dam. It looked about as inviting as a boil on the bum but it was closer to the motor so we decided to give it a night. It was hardly a flier but at least we did manage to extract a couple of carp from it. The first take I could not believe. There I was sitting behind the rods minding my own business and wondering what the hell we were doing there when "whoosh", one of my rods flew out of the rests and climbed into the sunset.

"Houston, we have a problem; abort mission."

The rods perched among the rocks in the difficult terrain.

From nowhere it re-entered the atmosphere, zoomed down and crashed into the margins. I fell over the rocks and crashed in after it, grabbing the butt as it flew like a torpedo across the surface. What a fish it turned out to be: six pounds of pure dynamite!

Just after dawn my left-hand rod decided to join the space programme, but I was alert to the situation, managing to grab it at the point of lift-off. Boy, did that fish go? Actually no; I wound it in like a wet sack. Still, it was good for the ego, a long yellow fish of twenty five pounds which at least proved that there were some good fish to go at.

It had hardly been all-action and I had the urge to be on the move. Unfortunately for us though a couple of local coppers decided to 'play chicken' with us on the dam wall. We'd obviously noticed them sitting

It went off like an Exocet missile! I couldn't believe it only weighed 8lb.

on their motorbikes, one either end of the dam, goggles pulled down as though they were auditioning for a Dirty Harry movie. Huffing and puffing and drenched in sweat we had just made the centre of the dam wall and stopped for a rest when they made their move. 'Vroom, vroom', the throttles revved and then they gave it the biggun, belting full speed down the dam wall towards us. Only feet away they diverged just like the Red Arrows, swerving either side of us.

"What else did your mam buy you for Christmas?" was my response.

We'd come to go fishing not play games so we loaded the jeep and set off across an unmarked track over the mountains to another lake on the map. We shouldn't have bothered. Some guard who thought he was Lee Van Cleef tailed us all the way. It was obvious we were not going to get any peace: we were being watched every inch of the way, so we did a U-turn and went back to the lake where we had started.

Arriving back we had a reception committee from the rejects for the Dirty Harry movie who informed us that we could not camp in one place for more than one night. In the circumstances there was only one thing to do, go and get absolutely lathered in the local village bars. No problem there; that's something I am genuinely good at. The rods did get out that night but it was little more than a token gesture. We were fishing blind, not knowing where the fish were as the only ones we had seen had been on the bank! I'm never confident in such a situation and my pessimism was borne out when we didn't get a sniff.

We were up early and all packed away by 8.00 a.m. With just 24 hours to go it was time to raid the supermarkets and empty their shelves of sweetcorn. Mission accomplished and loaded up with four crates of Little Green Giant we set off in search of an easy route to what was the obvious hot spot on the water. What a climb that proved to be! We made it there, and it was the hot spot for sure, but there was no easy way to it. Getting to the point that jutted out between the two inlets to the lake would have tested an Everest expedition. Even when we made it to the point there was no obvious place to set up: it was mostly sheer rock face, again with just the occasional shelf something like fifteen feet above the water. Anyone with conventional brolly and bivvy set-ups would have stood no chance of camping out. Luckily for us we'd taken along our dome tent which requites no pegging so is much more practical on rock or hard ground and only a fraction of the weight of a bivvy and brolly to carry. We'd also done the right thing in taking rod pods with us as there was literally nowhere a rod rest could have been driven in.

Time was running out so it was a case of piling the corn in as fast as we could, twenty four cans going in either side of the point onto the four-foot deep marginal shelf. For the first time on the trip I was confident. Sure enough no more than thirty minutes had passed

The only place to put the bivvy was in a hazardous position on top of a rock.

before we were interrupted from our sun-bathing and Annie was into an eighteen pound fully-scaled mirror.

Ten minutes and twenty knocks on the rod top later my clutch screamed and I'm rewarded with my first-ever twenty plus fully-scaled mirror. I couldn't have been more pleased. Non carp anglers think of us as single-species fanatics, but to me that is just not true: there are so many different carp to aim for. There are wildies, commons, mirrors, linears, fully-scaleds and leathers to start with, plus all the different strains. To my eyes the fully-scaled mirror is the most beautiful of the lot and it had long been an ambition of mine to catch a twenty plus. The fact that it took me nearly thirty years to achieve that ambition shows that in the waters I fish they are as rare as rocking horse dung.

Meanwhile, all the time I was playing the fish the tops of the other rods kept tapping. For sure some were line bites, but there was no way all of them could be. We'd caught enough of these fish to know that their mouths were as tough as old boots. Either the hooks weren't sharp enough or the leads weren't heavy enough to drive the hooks home. It was most likely a combination of both so off came the big forged hook and on went a size 6 Kamakatsu, which is about the sharpest hook I know. On the line we fixed two 3½oz leads. No, you've not misread it; that's seven ounces of lead fixed tight as hell to the swivel. Once the bait was in position the rod was bent into the lead for all it was worth and the line jammed hard in the butt clip. To say we were tight-lining would be an understatement! At one point a flock of swallows decided to land on the lines and we never even had a bleep!

From the moment the amended tackle setups went out it was all action with the Baitrunners screaming all over the place. We had planned to take some action pictures but it seemed that every moment was taken up with playing fish. It was almost on a par with the fishing at St. Genez. The odd single-figure fish was caught but most were mirrors of eighteen to twenty-three pounds, all hard-fighting fish with nice heavy-scale patterns. By today's standards none were monsters but it was a brilliant afternoon, the type to make you want to go out and celebrate on your last night. We'd caught enough carp in one afternoon to send us home happy; what happened from then on didn't really matter.

But before we could go out and celebrate the tent had to be erected. This was done on the only spot where it was remotely possible for a seagull to land, a small shelf that seemed to be about three feet square, eighteen feet above the water-line. We could only manage it by having the butts of our rods some two feet inside the tent door! We managed it, but with my back to the rock face I surveyed the scene: even goats couldn't have gone two abreast along that track. Two nightmares came straight into my head. One: how the hell could we make it up the mountain and down the precipice once we'd had a few – and we do tend to be sociable – and, two: if I needed a pee in the night, got up and fell over the rods I'd certainly be over the cliff face and it would be goodnight Rodney. But Annie seemed perfectly happy with the situation, so what the hell!

Well we had a great night out: did a bit of the old Flamenco dancing: did my bit on the old Spanish guitar: the old Apache always goes down well with anyone who can't play the guitar. When I've had a drink even I tend to imagine I'm one of those guitar greats, like Eric Clapton, Hank Williams or Bert Weedon! We had a good drink, ate loads of barbecued chicken and got interrogated by the secret policeman – who works in the city but lives in the village and pretends be a taxi driver – and all this by getting no further than some bloke's garage! Yes, definitely a very enjoyable night indeed.

What's more we safely made our way back along the wall of death, got both sets of rods cast out and settled back in a nice, happy frame of mind. I must admit to feeling disappointed when I woke up in bright sunshine and realised that there were no fish in the sacks. On the other hand I'd had a refreshing sleep, my bladder had held out, and I was still in one piece, which had to be regarded as a result in itself.

I tried to imagine I'm one of the guitar greats...

Annie's belief in boilies paid off with this personal best 38lb mirror caught late in the session.

Whilst answering nature's call I was surveying the swim for bubbles when a real lunker rolled some ten yards beyond our baited area. Time was running out for we had to be packed and away and on the road to Playa within the hour: all the same it seemed well worth while piling the rest of the corn in, hoping that the big fish might be attracted onto our baits. That done I climbed back into bed. The time flew by. My watch said five to eight; time to be packing up, when Annie's rod suddenly dipped over and the Baitrunner grudgingly started revolving. I couldn't believe it! There must have been at least ten pounds of corn out there yet some stupid carp had taken her boilie!

Annie leapt over me and was onto it like a shot, but was in bother from the start. Grit or something had got behind the spool and she was having great difficulty giving line. Perched precariously on the lip of the cliff edge I'm sure she would have been pulled in had I not been hanging onto her jacket. The scrap that ensued was more akin to tackling an SAS obstacle course than anything I'd ever seen before while fishing. The carp shot off into the snag-ridden inlet to our left but somehow my girl managed to follow it by clambering over the rocks and through the cacti.

It was funny; during the course of the fight every time the fish rolled it got bigger. It started off as a double, then it might have shaded twenty, then a big twenty, and so on. By the time it was netted our estimate had grown to a real lunker, and so it proved to be. It was a magnificent long scaley mirror, beating Annie's personal best by half a pound and weighing in at just over 38lb. Within the confines of that swim landing it had been quite an achievement.

The pictures were taken and everything was packed away in double quick time. I drove like a nutter down the mountain to Playa and we made it in time for our coach. We even had time for a drink. We had no money to pay for it, but that's another story...

Here We Go 17 Again...

As each season comes upon us some anglers set their goals for the year ahead. It may be to catch one particular fish, or to catch a string of twenties or thirties, or for others to beat their personal best. For myself I make no such aims. I've been at it long enough to know that when a target is set I usually fall flat on my face. If in the back of my mind there is something I would like to achieve I try to suppress it, and I certainly wouldn't go around telling people what I intend to do.

Instead with the start of each new season I just hope that we will catch some nice fish in pleasant surroundings and, above all, enjoy ourselves. Peace of mind and quality of life mean more than figures against our names. Having said that it would be wrong to imply that we'd fish anywhere; there has to be some sort of starting point. A water has to be capable of producing fish over thirty pounds for me to set my stall out and take it seriously. Not that I set my sights on those particular fish as I have always believed that if you fish correctly and catch a few the big ones will come along anyway. First learn to catch fish and the big fellas will take care of themselves.

I have a slightly different attitude towards my own lake in that the largest fish have been in the water quite a few years and consequently I have caught them several times. They may still come along, but I am not after catching them. I'd much prefer to catch some of the new fish coming through. Here we are lucky: there is a terrific head of fish, all of which have spawned in the lake and have now broken through to twenties. In the next couple of years it will be interesting to see which of the new fish are fliers. There are always a couple which, most likely because of their genetics, will grow much faster than the rest of their generation. To me these are exciting fish, ones which can make huge leaps in weight each year, as opposed to the old, large fish which do well if they increase by a couple of pounds. So despite the fact that I have fished the water on and off for something like eight years, I still find it interesting. Add to that the fact that it is not a difficult water and can therefore be used to tune up rigs, try out new ideas and refine the best dosage levels of flavours and oils, and it is not surprising that I start each season there. It is always good to get a few fish under your belt before tackling more difficult waters.

Rather than start with a long session each year I prefer to fish just afternoons and evenings using what I suppose is a semi-stalking approach. I walk round first trying to find some fish. Should I find more than one group then I pick out those that are either feeding, or look as though they are about to feed. You can generally pick these out: they

I settled in behind the cover on the shallows.

simply seem to move that bit quicker, and seem more alert. Something just tells you that they will take a bait if it is presented correctly. I might have an hour or two after them, at the most: if no takes materialise, or if one takes but scares away the rest of the shoal, I'll move on and try another spot.

As luck would have it on my first afternoon session several carp were moving around on the shallows, and although none looked particularly large it was a chance not to be missed to get the old rod bent again. When fish are moving well I don't see the point of putting out a bed of bait. Instead I prefer to anticipate their movements and place a bait where I expect them to end up. I'll scatter maybe half a dozen freebies around so that by the time they come across the hookbait they have a taste for it.

After casting out I had to wait no more than twenty minutes before the swinger whacked up and I was into my first carp of the season. It was only a baby, a small common around the twelve pound mark, but it gave a spirited account of itself. As I played it fish I'd been unaware of bolted off in all directions. The breeze was now lapping gently into the shallows from the southwest, creating perfect conditions for the water. In the circumstances I saw no point in moving, knowing it would not be very long before the fish returned.

I scattered another half a dozen baits around and sat back behind the cover, enjoying having the sun on my back for the first time that year. I'd started off with Livermix boilies, pepped up with 10ml of The Liver and 10ml of Amino Blend Supreme. It was a tried and proven bait on the water and I had complete confidence in it to produce a few takes. The baits were popped up about 1½" off the bottom on a size eight hook tied to 10lb breaking strain The Edge braid.

My rods were IMX 12ft, 3½lb test curve, which to many may seem very much over-gunned considering the size of fish I was likely to encounter and the fact that no distance casting was involved, yet I feel completely at home with them in any situation. Test curves frighten a lot of people, imagining that anything over 2½lb test curve has to be a brute stick. But it is not the test curve you should look for in a rod, it is the action. The 3½lb IMX has a complete through-action all the way to the butt: there is no lock-up which might make fishing light lines difficult, and fish can be confidently played beneath the rod tip without fear of breakage, or the hook pulling out. Unless you've experienced playing a fish on such a rod the sensation is hard to describe, but every movement of even a modest fish is transmitted right through the rod. If you need power, it's there; if you need sensitivity it is also there. Many reading this will think that I'm just doing another selling job on the rod here, which maybe I am, but I can assure you I would not be using them in close-in situations if I did not have every confidence in them.

Maybe three-quarters of an hour passed before the swinger first dropped back, then whacked up against the rod and the Baitrunner

A perfect start with a perfect linear of 21lb.

Here We Go Again.

What a way to start the day, 21½lb of perfect linear for Annie.

spool was spinning like a good un. The fish had shot off fast and had gone round a tree and into a reedbed before I was on it. Steady pressure told though and carefully it was brought back via the same route it had taken to go in. I was chuffed as hell with the fish, another baby, but quite a bit bigger, and an absolutely beautiful fish into the bargain. First session and a perfect linear going 21lb, and in all probability the first time it had graced the bank. Ten minutes later and I was in again: ain't life great? This time another baby, slightly smaller at 18lb, this one being a plump little mirror of the scattered variety: you know, one of those that look as though they've been covered in glue then had a couple of handfuls of scales thrown at them, the scales sticking all over the place at different angles.

Shortly after Annie arrived to pick me up. She was on her own, the kids staying with friends, so when she heard about the action she too decided to get the rods out. There was a quick visit to the pub for some food and refreshment before it was back to the lake to set up for the night.

Just after dawn the Optonic shrieked out and Annie was into her first carp of the season, and what a beauty it turned out to be; another immaculate linear, slightly larger than the one I'd caught, weighing 21½lb. First session out and twenties for both of us: can't be bad! We hurriedly photographed the fish before packing up and heading off for work.

The 23lb 12oz common taken on the drop!

Five days later I was back again. Again the wind was from a southerly direction, blowing into the islands. As I crept up behind the rushes the water was literally black with fish. I moved back and made my way round another rush bed. There lying on the ground was Ron, one of the syndicate members, watching fish hovering around his hookbaits. I don't like being disturbed so I left him to it and made my way across to the other side of the shallows, hoping that all the fish weren't congregated behind the islands. I need not have worried. Although there were far fewer fish moving along the opposite bank the carp that were there had their heads down and were feeding. It was magic: great big red clouds were colouring the water, while maybe half a dozen different patches of bubbles were rising enticingly to the surface. I couldn't get my tackle out quickly enough.

Tackle and bait were the same as the previous trip although I had taken along, almost as a precaution, a spray can of Bream Attractor. This was simply in the event that the carp were a bit timid on the Livermix combination which had, during the previous eighteen months, accounted for one hell of a lot of fish. If they were at all nervous of it a quick spray with the Bream Attractor and I'd have a different smelling bait. Not that I needed it! Half an hour after casting out I was in and my first 20lb plus common of the season was on the unhooking mat. They were feeding like crazy and it wasn't long before another linear was in the net, this one going 21lb. Just to see if it made any difference I sprayed one bait with the Bream Attractor and cast it between two small bushes sticking up off the sandbar where I could see fish bubbling. I hadn't even got the indicator on before the Baitrunner spool clicked into action. I think they would have taken anything I chucked at them. As it was the one on the end this time was another cracker of a common at 23lb 12oz. Half an hour passed before a 19lb common came to the net. What an afternoon's sport I was having, and despite all the eruptions in the swim the fish still kept feeding.

Around seven Annie and the kids arrived to pick me up. As I was still telling them what I'd had an Optonic sounded and I was in again.

The lake's new record common of 27lb.

Here We Go Again...

Straightaway I knew that it was a good fish. Not that it did anything spectacular; instead it just kind of held its ground which made it feel very heavy. In it came over the shallows, with a great bow wave following it. She was a big fat lump and on the scales broke the record for the lake for a common, going just over 27lb. An upper-double mirror completed the catch before we made our way home.

As I said at the start I never count on anything but with the start we'd made I couldn't help but think that we were in for a good season.

Return to the Valley

It may surprise some of you to know that although I've not fished the Colne Valley for six years I've kept up my ticket at two of the most popular of the valley's waters. This is most unusual for me for I must have let go about a dozen tickets over the last few years. For most of them the reasons why are not too difficult to explain. The first and most usual is that I've joined quite a few clubs over the years going chiefly on their reputation for large fish, or their potential to produce such fish, but on seeing these waters – well, I just didn't feel comfortable; didn't like the look of them, I suppose. Feeling happy just to be at a water is more important to me than catching big fish. The places where I've done exceptionally well have been where I've had both.

Savay was such a place. During the early years when it was basically just syndicate members I felt completely at home there. I rarely last two seasons on any water yet for four years I spent as much time as I could on that lake. I could never repeat the number of fish I caught there, not because I think it is harder – I don't see how it can be seeing there are miles more fish now than when I fished it since the restockings. It is still there to be done: Peter Broxup and John Harry have shown what you can do today if you are prepared to put the hours in, and good luck to them. But I could never make the early 80s commitment again. I remain a member because Savay is a water I love. At times it may get crowded but even if you don't catch the friends you are likely to bump into, Alf, Big Foot, The Tooth, Martini, The Brians, Roger and Kerry, would keep us amused.

Seriously though I think I would always fancy my chances on Savay. I've put more time in there than on any other water and every time I caught I used to think that they'd also be feeding in half a dozen other areas. In short there are not many places there where you aren't in with a chance. We don't get much free time these days but I'm sure there will come a time when I'll say to Annie, "Come on, let's fish Savay," and given a bit of a choice of swims I'd expect to catch. I might be disappointed and fail to catch, but so what? I've been disappointed before. I've never walked off Savay thinking "That's it, I'm done with the place." The fact that I haven't been there for over five years simply means that I've been too busy going to other places. The fact is that I've fished it as much as I could. It's just that I couldn't, if you get what I mean. It doesn't owe me a thing. I stay in because it's a great lake that I like to have the opportunity to fish, when I can.

The other water I've stayed in is a club lake where night fishing is not allowed. As such it is hard to get comfortable there, what with having to pack up each evening and then get up early to ensure a good swim. But these handicaps are also to the water's benefit as they prevent anyone living on the lake and hogging the going areas. It is a very fair system which gives everyone an equal chance – that is if you can get up

For many years I retained my ticket for Savay because it's a water I love.

in the morning, which isn't one of my strongest points! Obviously the local lads who can visit it regularly and get to know the moods of the water are most likely to fare the best but as each new day is a brand-new session I feel that when we fish there we're in which as much chance as anyone.

It is a water which still very much excites me. I had a few sessions there back in 1984 and had some really good fish up to 36lb, yet I never fished it enough to get bored with it, or feel that I knew it really well: I never caught enough for that to happen. In the intervening years the carp have really whacked on the weight; so much so that the water really represents our best chance of connecting with an English forty. I know there are plenty of other waters around today that can produce

A good thirty from the Club Water in the
early Eighties. I'd always been keen to return
and eventually we got round to it.

such fish, but it is back to the old story in that I can't feel comfortable on any of the others waters, a couple of which are really shit heaps. The added bonus for us is that the water is run as a family club. There are numerous other species and two really nice stretches of river close by to keep the children interested, plus a good pub nearby that does really good food. All of this means that we can spend a pleasant weekend together and be in with a chance of a really big fish.

Obviously living so far away, on a Friday evening it can mean a four-hour drive. I'm not in a position to visit the lake regularly but I am able to keep up with what is going on through Lee Jackson who fishes the water a couple of times a week through most of the season. Not that this really helps me on location because each day is different and the fish can be anywhere, but it does help to know if the fish are really on the move, if they are getting into the shallower areas, and what time of day appears to be the most productive.

We were into July before we – Annie, me and the dogs (can't forget them, they won't allow you to!) were able to make our first trip. The last leg of the journey along the M25 was horrendous and although we got to the lake a good hour and a half before packing up time I was too bog-eyed and in no fit state to get the rods out. Instead we just walked round, generally looking and talking to the anglers present. As luck would have it a 19-pounder was landed as we arrived and it was clear that the area housing many small islands had quite a few fish moving around. We got chatting to Colin Booker who suggested a small swim by the car park would be a good bet for the following day, and as it was in the general area we fancied anyway we made up our minds to give it a go the following morning. After whipping down to the Kentucky for supper (it must be the only one in the UK that never has any chicken!) and giving the dogs a walk along the canal towpath we got our heads down in the camper, ready for an early start.

How we made it I'll never know but somehow 3.30 a.m. saw us queuing up at the gate like a right pair of keenies. None of the regulars seemed bothered with the area we intended fishing – which, on reflection should have told us something – so bleary-eyed in the half light we set up our swim. Annie fished one rod down the margins to her left while her other rod was cast onto a shallow gravel bar about twenty yards out which had a patch of rushes on it. My left-hand rod was cast just short of an area of snags between two islands, while my right-hand rod was fished down the margins to my right. For bait we stuck with my Liver Mix/Liquid Liver and ABS combination that had served us so well everywhere else we had fished in the previous couple of years. We both chose to fish double boilie bottom baits on one rod with a pop-up on the other.

For the first hour or so we watched hard, alert for any movement of fish, but then tiredness took a hold and soon we nodded off on the bedchairs. It had just gone ten when I awoke: all was still, the air nice and warm and I was surprised that we'd had no signs of action

The Club water at dawn, although making it onto the bank in time for dawn on the day-only venue was sometimes a struggle!

The dogs always went along. They wouldn't have had it any other way!

considering the favourable conditions. For some reason Annie didn't feel happy with her margin rod, fearing the bait might be in weed, and decided on a recast. As her bait hit the water the swim erupted with at least half-a-dozen good carp bow-waving off in all directions. Without a doubt they had been on her bait. If only she had decided not to recast I'm sure she would have had one. They were the last fish we saw that day. From there on in it was frustration all the way. If it wasn't coots or tufties the swans would be on the bait. We fished on till the death but the birds beat us.

It was nearly midnight by the time we'd had a meal, walked the dogs and got our heads down. Three-thirty came – but I didn't see it! Annie woke me at five-thirty but I was still too shattered to get up. It was ten-thirty before we made our way up the bank! Any early morning activity was well over, besides which all the likely-looking swims were taken. As we had to be off by two in the afternoon our only real chance seemed to be to pick a swim in the middle of the lake, put a few baits down and hope that some time during our short stay a fish or two might come across them. In the event I don't think any did as we packed up at two without as much as a bleep! First session and we'd blanked, but we'd been close. If only Annie hadn't decided on that recast...

The following weekend we were back again, arriving just before dark on the Friday evening. A quick walk round revealed a few fish moving between the far end of the lake and the islands. The forecast for the following day was for light winds with a chance of some rain, in short nothing spectacular to move the fish from where they were already. I decided to fish The Point where the lake narrows down: some time during the day a fish or two was bound to pass through. I only hoped that this time I could make the early morning call.

Actually I was so excited that I don't think I slept at all. At two-thirty I was up making a flask and getting everything ready. By three o'clock I was first in the queue by the gate. As Gary was with us on this trip Annie elected to have a lay-in while he slept, and then make a start when he was awake. Making my way through the marsh area leading to the Point I got absolutely soaked. Over the years I'd been that accustomed to either bivvying up or fishing afternoons and evenings that I'd forgotten how heavy and just how wet the early-morning dew can be and had not gone prepared. Soaked or not it was magic to be at the lake again in the half light leading up to dawn. It really is an exciting time wishing and hoping, as the light gains strength, that you are going to witness a swim alive with carp.

As it became lighter it became clear that I was going to see no such spectacle, although there was enough movement in the water to make me confident of a result some time during the day. As soon as I could I set about plumbing the swim. I learnt less about the depth than I did about the density of the weed! It was murder just trying to wind the marker float in. Each retrieve brought with it a great mass of weed, some forms of which are rarely found in lakes and generally only inhabit well oxygenated streams or rivers. The presence of such weeds bares witness to the quality and oxygen content of the water. Small wonder that the carp in the lake are growing so well.

It seemed to take forever before I found anywhere where I could confidently present a bait but eventually I found a couple of spots. I had already decided to stick the day out in the swim: early morning starts give me neither the energy nor the inclination to go chasing around! I was convinced that some time or other carp would have to pass through. I set up the swim accordingly, baiting quite heavily with the Liver Mix boilies, determined that when the fish did come through there was no way that they'd miss the baits. Oh, the best laid plans of mice and men... I hadn't reckoned on the tufties and coots but in they came and mopped the lot up.

"Go away you naughty little fluffy fellows," I shouted at them, but they took not a scrap of notice. Something to do with the pecking order, I suppose...

Annie arrived about 8.30 to find me fast asleep beneath the coverall as rain had started falling some time around 6.30. I'm always pleased to see her but on this occasion more so than usual as she had a big flask in her hand and a carrier bag full of egg and bacon rolls. They went down a treat, despite the fact that I had to share them with two begging dogs. The sun finally broke through and it was really relaxing as Annie and I nodded off on the bedchairs while Gary enjoyed himself fly fishing for chub on the nearby River Colne.

Come lunch time we were feeling peckish again and retired to the local pub. While Annie and I enjoyed our food Gary was feeding up a couple of big chub he had found beneath a footbridge that spanned a small tributary of the Colne. He was dying to get his rod out but in the circumstances, being on private land, we had to hold him back. I felt a bit guilty about this as I knew exactly how he felt.

There seemed to be no need to rush so I guess it must have been about three by the time we were back in the swim. Nothing seemed to be stirring but I felt sure that some time during the evening a carp or two would be sure to move through. After the morning's attentions from the tufties and coots we doubted if any bait was left out and so decided to bait up quite heavily again with about a kilo of bait going into two areas. We should have known better for within minutes our feathered friends once again flew in for their free meal. As the first one dived down a bow wave moved off along the first gravel bar twenty yards out. It was the same old story; the carp angler's nightmare. Carp in themselves are not too difficult to catch, it's solving the problems that surround fishing for them that pose the questions. Short of napalm I don't know the answer to this one: it surely is the most frustrating element of carp fishing. In this case the problem was even more exaggerated because of the time it had taken to find a spot to present a bait.

And yet despite the problems I felt even more confident. The fact that one carp had been in the swim led me to believe, rightly or wrongly, that there were still a few baits out there and that at least one fish had a taste for them. When that is the case it will usually be back for more. We just had to hope it - or they - would return before we had to leave the water.

To others looking on it probably seemed stupid for us to be rebaiting every couple of hours as all it seemed to do was encourage the birds even more, but I felt it was the only way I could ensure that at least some baits remained in the swim. What it certainly ensured was that the swinger indicators were never still: they were up and down like a fiddler's elbow.

About eight in the evening the swans moved in and scared off the tufties and coots. I wasn't sure what was worse! I could see the big cob moving along the close in gravel bar in the direction of my left-hand bait. I didn't want to move it, but at the same time I didn't want to get hooked into Hissing Sid. I left it right till the last minute hoping he might just miss the bait but sure enough, down he went. The swinger crept to the rod, the line pinged out of the clip and the Baitrunner went into overdrive – which was all a bit puzzling because the swan hadn't moved from the spot!

I leapt for the rod and bent into the unknown culprit, not knowing what to expect. I didn't know what I'd hit into: a fish for sure but at first the fight was very un-carp-like, being very fast and jerky with the fish changing direction every few seconds. I told Annie that it was either a big tench, a pike or a small carp. That was about all I could fathom out but after two or three minutes the fish rolled and I said:

"Well at least it's a carp. Only a small one, but it's a carp."

A couple more minutes passed and Annie caught sight of it.

"It's not that small," she said, to which I responded, "Well it might make a nice double."

The fight it gave belied my estimations though and it probably took a good ten minutes before Annie slid the net under it. Even then, looking down into the net I was convinced it was a big double, but secretly hoped it might make twenty.

"It's a big one," yelled Annie, heaving up the mesh before lowering it onto the unhooking mat. Sure enough it was and at 31lb had made our decision to return to the Valley well worthwhile. We had no more takes that evening. Quite honestly I wasn't too bothered for myself but it would have been nice if Annie had caught one. The following morning we were up bright and early and fished the same swim until about eleven when it was time to pack up and make the long journey home.

As I write we've not managed to get back to the water since that trip. What breaks we've had we have taken in France. But it was good to be back on the venue, and back in the Valley again, and we are talking about trying to put a bit more time in there next season. Maybe this time it will be Annie's turn: after all she has usually managed a big fish or two from every other water we have visited. If we manage to get back I'm sure her turn will come.

Quite clearly it wasn't a swan.

Every Picture Tells a Story

Way back in '72 on a stinking hot July afternoon I was walking round the old carp pool at Woldale. Back then the water was considered as second only to Redmire, having been made famous by Maurice Ingham, Dick Walker and the Carp Catchers Club back in the 1950s. The water is, for the most part, very shallow, like Redmire being formed by the damming of a small stream. In the extreme heat most of the carp could clearly be seen lying up in the weed. The largest fish on view was less than a yard from the bank and it was an easy job to creep up through the long bankside grass and observe the fish from close quarters.

It soon became evident that the fish was feeding on weed! It would push its head into a clump of thick elodea (Canadian pondweed) and shake it. Bits of weed would then break away and as they slowly sank the carp would suck them in and eat the small pieces. I watched for maybe half an hour, completely mesmerised by it all, before I realised that the carp was perfectly catchable.

Shooting back to the car I picked up a rod and landing net then crept back to my former position. The old carp was still munching away, oblivious of me. Impaling a small two-inch piece of weed on the hook with a small shot three inches above it I gently lowered the morsel right down in front of the carp. As it slowly sank past the carp's snout its gills opened and she sucked the bait straight in. The fight wasn't spectacular due to the amount of weed about and she was soon on the bank. She weighed 15½lb and was identified as a fish caught by Fred J. Taylor at the same weight, nearly twenty years previously, the picture of that capture still adorning the wall of the estate cottage.

* * *

I'd had a terrific afternoon's sport, catching five carp in just two hours, all on maggots, the largest of which just touched thirty. It was only a short session as I had an urgent appointment. I'd baited a clear bowl-like area really heavily with maggots and hemp and I couldn't resist a look from a high vantage point to see if any fish were still there. My eyes nearly popped out! There, still grubbing about, was the biggest carp I'd ever seen in the lake, along with another fish that looked to be an upper twenty. There also appeared to be what I thought was a big roach in attendance.

Appointment or not I had to have one last cast. The bait had hardly settled and while I was attaching the bobbin the line was pulled from my hand. I struck, expecting all hell to let loose: instead the roach came flapping in – only it wasn't a roach but a lovely little carp. My mate Vic turned up as I left and cast across to the bowl. He rang me in the morning: he'd caught the two remaining fish, both mirrors at 33lb 12oz and 27lb 12oz.

* * *

We'd been catching well and were rapidly running out of bait. Searching through the van I found some small Aminoblend baits from the year before. They had dried out completely and were as hard as marbles. I doubted if they would be acceptable to the fish but as we had little else left by way of bait I decided to try one, out of desperation really. Half an hour later the 'marble' was picked up, resulting in a beautiful 25lb fully-scaled mirror. We salvaged the other baits that were left in the bottom of the cupboard and every one produced a carp. Since that day I always dehydrate my baits for session fishing.

* * *

Making my way back from the Colne bank at Savay towards the car park I stopped for a rest and a smoke in the Birches. It looked good, inviting somehow, so I decided to cast out, just for a couple of hours. Two baits were soon out, one at thirty yards and the other at about seventy, both areas having produced well for me in the past.

My attention kept being drawn to the overhanging tree to my right. Often in the past, particularly during the afternoon, carp would lie up amongst the branches that reached out into the water. I felt that I had to have a bait there, but I didn't want to disturb the other rods as they were in two good areas.

Now there was a two-rod rule during the day, so I had to be a bit crafty. After casting out a rod to the tree I then broke it down and hid it under the holdall, which was lying on the floor. No sooner had that task been completed than down the path came a certain bailiff who was notorious for his zealous application of the rules. He started chatting and all the time I'm thinking, "I wish he'd bugger off."

All of a sudden he said, "What's that noise?"

Looking down I saw the holdall leaping up and down! The bailiff looked at me and said, "I think I'd better be going!"

With that he turned his back and left me to it. The stroke rod had produced a lovely 20lb+ mirror!

* * *

November at Redmire: I don't know if that constitutes winter-time but it was bloody cold. At that time most of the guys in the syndicate stopped fishing in September and with no bait going in the carp easily went into a torpid state as the temperatures dropped. The fishing was very hard. I tried all I knew but could get no response. I really did think that the fish were laid up for the winter. Not wanting to flog a dead horse I decided to pack up and threw my remaining bait, a few mini-maples, tares and hemp in off the dam wall.

Now packing up is no quick job and it was probably an hour later that I crossed the stile and made my way back across the dam wall to the car park under the trees. Taking a last look across the lake I spotted a few bubbles coming up from the area where I'd recently thrown the bait in. I doubted if carp were responsible but decided to give it another hour, just using one rod.

There was one little problem though; I'd no bait! Searching around on the dam wall I salvaged a few grains of hemp. In the bottom of my tackle box were a handful of very strong size twelve stainless steel hooks. Onto one of these I managed to impale three grains of hemp, after splitting a dozen or so grains in the attempt. The bubbles were close in and I was able to lower the bait into the centre of them. Not

long after that I got a really slow, twitchy take. It was so slow I wasn't sure if it was a take or not but struck all the same – and I was in.

Quite a fight followed but the little hook held solid and this splendid common found its way into the net. It had been hooked through the tip of its barbule.

* * *

The BBC Breakfast Television crew turned up at Savay on opening night. I knew that they were there but was unprepared when a camera and microphone were thrust into my bivvy at the crack of dawn. I don't know who was more shocked, me or the viewers. As luck would have it out of all the anglers on the lake (and it was pretty crowded as you might expect on opening night) they chose the three who most liked a drink, me, Tony Abbott and Dave Orriss. No wonder the general public think that all carp anglers are mad!

Well they kept asking why no one was catching anything and I kept telling them that 7.30 a.m. till 10.00 a.m. was the time when it would happen. That was no good, they said, they had to be back in the studio for 7.30 as the film was due to be shown on TV around 8.00 a.m. Ironically between 7.30 and 9.00 three carp were caught, all of which were mid-twenties. They fell to the rough crew, me, Orris and Abbott. My contribution was a mid-twenty mirror.

* * *

Do you remember the hurricane which swept through the south of England, snapping trees off at their roots and causing all kinds of devastation? Well we were out on the English Channel in that, scared to hell and dodging flying vomit all night long. Never have I been so glad to get off a ferry. It was so rough we were still seasick two days later. The hurricane blew on over Brittany and during the first night the brolly was destroyed. It was an impossible task to keep the rods in the rests.

For three days we really struggled. Carp fishing hadn't really taken off in France at that time and with no bait going in to keep them on the move the carp had settled into their winter quarters. Only problem was, we didn't know where their winter quarters were: that is until with just twenty-four hours to go to the end of the trip one popped its head out. That was a mistake on its part for I had five fish

out in those twenty-four hours, three of which were thirties, The Beast being the best of them. Incidentally the bait was flavoured with Mega Tutti Frutti EA, a great flavour all year round but particularly effective in winter.

* * *

There are two stories in one here, really. The previous two seasons I had caught a large number of big carp, with sixteen fish over 35lb, without catching a forty pounder. The frustrating thing was that a number of these fish, including the big common I'd caught at 39lb 12oz, had appeared in papers and magazines – with other anglers – at weights well over forty pounds. Well one morning, while fishing in the Seine Valley I caught a carp which I knew was a good thirty. Wanting someone to photograph it I went round to some lads from Berkshire and told them of the catch. Round to the swim they came and weighed

the fish on my digital scales. I couldn't believe it: 29½lb they read. One of the lads suggested that we weigh it on his Reuben Heaton scales, which we did: the needle indicated 33lb!

Relating this story to John Van Eck he took my scales from their box and started reading the leaflet inside. John asked me if I'd read the leaflet, to which I replied that I hadn't

"Well you should," said John, "it says here that these scales are accurate to plus or minus ten percent. That's four pounds on a forty!"

The digital scales were unceremoniously dumped in the bin.

One night on our next trip John was having a drink with us when I connected with a fish. John did the netting for me and, looking down at the enormous length of the fish, said:

"You've got that forty."

However it had less fat on it than a cold chip and weighed 38lb 8oz.

* * *

For things to go right so many things have to fall into place. For things to go wrong only one thing can throw a spanner in the works and balls up all your plans. When the water you fish is a 600-mile drive away your fate really is in the lap of the gods. I missed our intended ferry, which meant a delay of an hour. This was to prove highly significant. We'd fished our destination water before from all positions round the lake and it was the most hot-spotted water I'd ever fished. You had to be in one of the three best swims or you really struggled to even get a run.

On arriving at the lake I was gutted; all three swims were taken. In fact in the best swim of all the guy was just setting up, having arrived minutes before us. From a fishing point of view missing that ferry had ruined the whole trip. We knew from experience that the available bank space was a waste of time under all but the most extreme conditions. For four days I didn't even get the rods out then one afternoon one hell of a storm blew up. There was thunder, lightning, lashing rain, and waves three-feet high lashing the bank that was unoccupied. It was my only chance so out came the rods.

Sure enough in the middle of the night they turned up, amongst them a beautiful 33lb common, the last good fish of my hairy period! Four other commons, two of which were twenties, were also landed. The furthest bait from the bank was fished at a range of ten yards, two of the fish coming from under the rod top.

Just Mates

Fast forward to 12th April 2009. I was fast asleep dreaming about a huge lake I'd come across in the mountains of the Massif Centrale in France many, many years before. It was one I'd never fished, largely because I couldn't weigh up any means of access down to the waterside, other than abseiling! It was a dream that I'd had several times before, always trying to overcome the problems. Yet the funny thing was it wasn't something I ever thought about in the daytime. Weird. So there I was clambering my way down this rope when the phone rang and I fought my way out of the dream. Putting the light on I glanced at the clock: it was four in the morning. Who on earth would ring me at that time?

My first thought was that it must be bad news from my brother Dave in New Zealand. I knew that he had been very ill, but from what I'd heard I thought that he was well on the mend. Leaping out of bed, my mind full of trepidation, I picked up the phone.

"Who is it?" I asked nervously.

"It's me," replied the voice on the other end of the line.

"And who the hell is me?" I asked.

"It's me, Johnny."

"Who?"

"Johnny Allen," came the reply.

Now I hadn't seen Johnny for over twenty years, the last time being when he came up to Louth to stay with Annie and me and have a few jars. At that time Johnny had just broken up with his lady and was thoroughly despondent with life: in his own words, "Pissed off". He had sold his pad, he said, and was leaving the country and going off, travelling the world. He wasn't sure if he'd ever be back again. Like me John was a music freak and wanted me to have his entire record collection, which I was very grateful for as there were some absolute classics among them. The following morning when Annie and I woke up Johnny had gone. Where he had gone I didn't know but I surmised that Cassien would be his first port of call. Now here he was again, twenty years on, at four in the morning, on the other end of the line!

"How are you Johnny?" I asked "How are you keeping?"

"Never better mate! I'm having the time of my life. Get yourself out here."

I have to say that from the sound of his voice he was three sheets to the wind; well and truly intoxicated.

"Where are you then mate?" I asked, now interested and thinking that he may have discovered a new equivalent of Cassien, or even better.

"Thailand, mate, Thailand. It's the best place on earth. Get yourself out here."

I made a few quite legitimate excuses as to why I couldn't but Johnny

Johnny Allen in his circuit-water carp-fishing days pictured here with Mary from Wraysbury.

was having none of it. He was adamant that I get on the next plane to Thailand!

"Look, Stuart (Gilham) has said that you can have a free holiday at his lake. It's fabulous. I had a two-hundred pounder last week. Lee's (Jackson) been out: Maylin's been out. Ask them. It's fabulous I promise you. Look, if you're hard up I'll even pay your air fare and pick you up at Bangkok airport. You've got to come mate, you've got to come."

I couldn't get a word in during his tirade, punctuated by hiccups. He went off on one again!

"Look Rod, the weather's fantastic, the whole country's fantastic, the fishing is brilliant with fish bigger than anything you have ever dreamed of. I'm telling you the truth. You always liked a curry and the food out here is absolutely brilliant, the best I've had anywhere in the world. And the women... Oh the women man; you would not believe it. Even an ugly old bugger like you could walk round with the most beautiful girl in the world on his arm..." he paused for a moment, then added, "...providing you've got a few bob in your back pocket. Look mate I'm running out of credit on the phone. Please get yourself out here. If you don't come before you die you'll regret it for the rest of your life."

Then he was gone. I felt there was a bit of a contradiction at the end of his ramblings and had to think about what he'd said. In fact I still do! He rang off and I was left to stumble back to bed. I tried to get back into my dream but instead found myself being chased by an elephant through a marketplace in some oriental city.

Mally wasn't his usual self on the long drive through Belgium and France. Every hour or so we had to stop and Mally would either take a walk or go to the loo. His legs seemed stiff, his back seemed stiff, but he made no reference to the pain he was clearly suffering. The journey which we had made several times before took much longer than usual. We had departed from our overnight ferry promptly at 9.00 a.m. at the port of Zeebrugge in Belgium but didn't arrive at the small town close to our destination lake until close to six in the evening.

Our first port of call was the local supermarket to stock up on provisions for our week ahead. Normally we buy nothing fancy, preferring to live on cereals and fruit in the mornings and a baguette each – which could be filled with all manner of things, including meat, fish, sardines and fish fingers and my occasional weakness, bananas and condensed milk – for our evening meal. In between our healthy meals for the week we'd eat snacks; cheese, cakes and biscuits, often accompanied

Mally clearly wasn't himself that trip...

by a glass of pastis. Our opinion was, and still is, that you haven't really sampled the delights of France unless you have enjoyed pastis. Really we had very few items to pick up, but even that took longer than usual. Mally was clearly suffering and was literally shuffling around the hall, seemingly held up by the shopping trolley.

As we came through the check-out Mally noticed a large pharmacy to our right, attached to the supermarket. He told me to stop and wait as he needed to go to the said pharmacy. I stood by the door, leaning on the trolley, while Mally went in. It was clear that he was looking around for something, but not finding it. I had no idea what he was seeking although it later transpired that he was looking for a male assistant. The thought "Once a sailor, always a sailor," flashed through my mind.

He looked suspicious, almost furtive. Even the parrot permanently on his shoulder was looking pensive, its head turning round through a full 360° looking for hidden surveillance cameras. The two of them were so close it was as though the bird knew everything that was going through Mally's mind. Then disaster struck. The staff behind the counter had all been watching them and their suspicious movements. A young female assistant approached him enquiring as to what he was looking for.

Now to understand the following conversation it helps if you have a degree in languages. My French isn't that bad, but with Mally I have to have an interpreter for any meaningful exchange. As the crow flies Mally and I probably live no more than fifty miles away from each other. If the crow's had a drink, or gets stuck on the motorway into Hull, it seems closer to eighty miles. Between us is the River Humber. It isn't a massive river, being only four miles wide at high tide, even in its estuary, yet this divide has clearly created a language barrier. The dialects of Hull and Lincolnshire are so different that outsiders could believe that we were from two different countries.

In our formative years when we were kids growing up in the middle of a thriving fishing industry Hull and Grimsby were the two largest fishing ports in the world. For the anoraks among you people from my old town of Grimsby, my birthplace, hated being called Codheads, although for some wherever we go this is how we are sometimes referred to. The good people of Hull – always referred to in Grimsby as Hully Gullies – didn't like it either! Hull was the capital of the cod industry. Grimsby was where every trawler stuffed to the boards with haddock headed for. But I guess 'Haddockhead' didn't trip off the tongue as easily as 'Codhead' and as a result both communities somehow, in the eyes of others, got lumped together. But there was always rivalry between the two banks of the Humber as to which port was doing best, which one had landed the biggest tonnage of the year, and so on.

But for all that both sides had a great respect for each other. Why else would all the deckhands and deckie learners, resplendent in their baggy pleated suits, very often in pink, lime green, sky blue or blood orange red go across the river? It was two-way traffic on a Saturday night for a drink and, one or the other, a woman or a scrap. Both sides were pretty much the same really; there was just this language barrier between us. I'm serious. I've been waiting for a 'fern curl' (phone call) from Mally for weeks now!

I've digressed. Back to the pharmacy, where the members of the staff were terrified they were going to be held up by a hobbling man and his parrot. (To be fair the parrot did look as though it could get vicious!) Finally a trembling shop assistant approached Mally.

"Excuse me sir, may I help you?"

Mally pretended not to hear, still scanning the shop for signs of a male assistant. The girl tried again.

"May I help you sir?"

I could see the old panic in Mally's eyes. The assistant tried once more before Mally cracked and tried the old bluff ploy. From hereon in Mally's dialogue is from a language yet to be deciphered.

"Sorry. Je suis Anglais. English. No parlez Francais," said Mally, shrugging his shoulders, and almost dislodging his parrot whilst doing so.

"But sir I am speaking English," replied the assistant.

This obviously threw Mally. For my part, listening from the open door, I couldn't help thinking, "You may be speaking English, dear, but can you speak Hully Gulley?"

I could see Mally's mind ticking over. What devilish ploy would he come up with next, I wondered? Meanwhile the parrot was getting bored, hopping from shoulder to shoulder, looking severely agitated. At any moment I expected it to say, "Stick 'em up; hands up!"

Mally tried a new ploy. Turning to the young assistant he said:

"Now it is obvious that you don't speak English I will talk to you in French."

The girl looked puzzled but hung on in there.

"Avez vous un homme?" asked Mally, a very rough translation being "Have you a man?" meaning "Have you a male assistant?"

The girl panicked and replied in English.

"Yes, yes, yes, I have a man, a very big man."

Mally, thinking that he was finally getting somewhere, followed through.

"Where is he? I want to speak to him, you understand, parlez avec man."

"Oh, he is in the gym, big man, big muscles," came the reply.

It seemed to suddenly click with Mally that there was no male assistant available. He was in pain and had to bite the bullet and explain to the girl what he was trying to find.

"You understand my French?" He asked the girl.

She nodded. Head in hand, with the other one close to his lips (That's two hands. Mally hasn't got two heads, although he did have three once, on the night of the Millennium party.) Mally whispered, shyly, being almost bashful:

"Avez vous, mademoiselley (rhymed with jelly), le preparation pour..." he hesitated for a while seemingly embarrassed before summoning up the courage to come out with it, "...pour, er, um, le Michael Miles?"

"The preparation for Michael Miles, monsieur, I do not understand," said the girl, understandably puzzled.

Mally was having to dig deeper, if you'll pardon the pun, when in walked a smart young man who obviously worked there and had returned from his break. He sensed that there was tension in the air, went over to the staff behind the counter and asked, obviously in French, what the problem was. The man listened to what was said then walked towards Mally and the young girl assistant. In perfect English, with a slight German accent he asked:

"What is the problem sir? May I be of assistance?"

"May I have a word with you in private?" asked our man, while the bloke ushered the long-suffering girl assistant away.

"What is the problem?"

"The old Michael Miles are giving me some right jip. Have you got any cream for the old bullets?" his voice was quiet but his eyes were pleading.

"Le Michael Miles, monsieur? I do not understand."

Mally was at the end of his tether. Crouching down and pointing at his anus, he cracked.

"The Michael Miles; the Johnny Giles; the Nobby Stiles. My bloody piles are killing me."

"Oh, now I understand, monsieur," said the assistant.

"Thank cluck for that," said the parrot.

The man turned and walked over to the counter, saying in French, so I'll tell it in English:

"OK everybody, panic over. Have we any Preparation H for the gentleman?"

Everyone let out a huge sigh of relief and relaxed. Purchase duly made we left the shop and Mally was given a round of applause!

It has often occurred to me that if Mally worked on his paunch a bit, shaved his head and got rid of that parrot, from the back he would be a dead ringer for Paul Woods of Planet Carp fame. In many ways they are very alike. They are both passionate in what they believe in, even when there is conclusive proof that they could possibly be wrong! These guys make Vlad the Impaler look like a Liberal Democrat. There is right, and everything else is wrong, with nothing in between, which, in principle I basically agree with. It is just in the way we go about settling problems where I don't see eye to eye with them. These lads make Rambo look like a candidate for the Green Party. Maybe Mally has a slightly softer side to him, Paul being the original 'Muscles from Brussels', while Mally is more like 'mussels with truffles.'

Mally and I had been on the Orient for two weeks when Paul

Paul Woods with a big kipper at 60lb+ from a successful trip to Cassien.

arrived to join us for a session. The two had never met before and I was fully expecting the clash of the Titans, but much to my surprise they got on like a house on fire. Both have a wonderful sense of humour and a constant stream of one-liners bounced back and forth between them. We were in mid-October and the water level was dropping by the minute. The fishing was very difficult and you really had to know where to position your hookbaits to have any success at all, the most productive areas being to the left of the beach by Mesnil harbour, familiarly known as Bivvy City. Actually by that time of year 'beach' was the wrong description. We had long since passed the sand, gravel and broken tiles areas and were, by then, set up in thick mud which came

**Sharing an early morning brew with a cardboard
cut-out of Mally on the Orient.**

almost up to our knees.

Late one afternoon a party of six German anglers turned up. On seeing that only the shallow water close to the Mesnil harbour wall was available they decided to go elsewhere and have a look round the lake for somewhere that would offer them a better chance. As darkness moved in some good six hundred yards out we could see snags sticking out of the water as a gravel bar which we knew nothing about was slowly being exposed.

We had a very pleasant evening. Mally whipped off into the village and brought back a ready-cooked chicken, straight off the spit, which we broke into small portions and dropped into the simmering pot of curry that I had on the go. The curry was accompanied by the obligatory long glass of pastis, which went down like nectar. Bellies full, pots in the lake to let the lapping waves wash them, it was out with the guitars and sing-song time. Woodsy was a revelation. Not only did he know the old blues and soul classics that form the main part of 'MalRod's' repertoire but also seemed to know countless humorous songs from musicals and from the old music halls. He was like a cross between Gilbert and Sullivan, Max Miller, Stanley Holloway and George Formby. Now I am not the world's best guitarist but I can generally get away with bluffing it. It's not difficult. You just drop everything into the key of C and miss out any difficult chords! We had a great evening with the two of them having me in stitches. Eventually I drifted off to sleep listening to Mally's rendition of Bob Marley's 'No woman, no cry', with the guitar left on auto pilot.

Come the dawn it was a typical October morning for that part of France, namely thick fog. None of us had had any signs of action so I turned over and went back to sleep for another couple of hours, waiting for the fog to clear. It must have been around ten when I awoke to the sound of what I thought was shouting, but turned out to be singing.

The fog had cleared and the water had dropped at least a foot from the previous evening. That gravel bar that had recently betrayed its presence way out in the middle of the lake was no longer a gravel bar and was now a fully-fledged island. What's more under cover of darkness and early morning fog it had been occupied by the group of Germans we had met the night before. It was no problem to me. They were 600 yards away. But Woodsy and Mally felt very differently about the Germans' perceived intrusion on 'our' territory and were responding accordingly. They were marching up and down our beach and – I hope not with rage but in light-hearted humour – at the top of their voices they were singing their version of the theme from Dad's Army!

"Who do you think you are kidding Mr. Hitler,
If you think old England's done?
We are the boys who will stop your little game,

We've had carp from the Orient and the Seine.
Mr. Mall goes off to work on the eight twenty eight,
But he comes home at night and he's ready with his bait.
So who do you think you are kidding Mr. Hitler,
If you think old England's done?"
Encore.

Trying to make a living in Europe this was something I could have done without, but naturally I couldn't stop laughing! The following day three of the Germans came round, asking how we had done, and what all the fuss was about the previous morning. Luckily the sound hadn't carried across the vast acreage of water between us. But the lads had been watched through the binoculars from the island, and I can only put the comments that followed from the Germans down to the sun striking Paul's shaven head.

Paul Woods

"You all looked excited. It looked like someone was marching up and down with a German helmet on."

I rest my case.

Mark Lawson had been a bit of a fan of me and my carp baits for several years. A young lad mad on carp fishing he would write to me every couple of weeks trying to gain an edge from the wise one's wisdom. It became a two way thing: he was a young carp angler, as keen as mustard, and I needed good proper fieldtesters to try out my products and give me an honest assessment. Although we had never met before the first time we fished together was at Mark's invitation. He had read most of my articles and knew that in addition to carp fishing I enjoyed beach casting for cod in the winter months. I was invited to join him for a beach-fishing session.

The drive down to the Sussex coast was horrendous, with lashing rain, non-stop. The only music I had in the old Renault 4 was Sade's debut album. Now depending on your taste she might have seemed beautiful, even fanciable, but it was music to cut your throat to!

I met Mark and his father at a pub just outside the small town of Battle. We had arranged to meet at this destination because they knew that I liked a pint, and this pub, they assured me, served the best pint in the area. Well, they say that beauty is in the eyes of the consumer and they loved it, eagerly extolling its virtues. I thought it was horrible; flat as a pancake. It was as though they had poured it the night before and left it on the bar to settle. A few of those and I knew it would be head down the big trombone time.

I slept heavily that night on Mark's settee, not waking till Mark walked through the door laden with carrier bags.

"I've been out to get the breakfast," he said, "I hope you are hungry."

Now I have worked all round the United Kingdom, even for a short time in the Persian Gulf, but I have never seen a breakfast the size of this one. Having run a lake for many years one of the rules is that you have to pass an initiation ceremony: you have to finish a Ten Acres' (a café close to the lake) double breakfast. Believe me that is some task, but what Mark put before me that morning would have defied the combined knowledge of Galileo, Einstein and my Uncle Louie in figuring out how it could be consumed at one sitting. On a plate normally reserved for the Christmas turkey Mark served me up the following gastronomic delight. Served on a bed of four rounds of fried bread, cooked in beef dripping (none of that healthy muck!) came the following:

First of all a bed of tomatoes, the proper stuff, straight out of a tin; second, a bed of curried baked beans with sultanas; third four rashers of fatty bacon; fourth, four sausages, the size of which any man would have been proud; fifth, six black puddings; sixth, two sunny side up over and under eggs; seventh, a small 7oz sirloin steak; eighth – and it was getting daft now – half a pound of kidneys. Ninth came Mark's coup de gras; half a pound of sweetbreads, which was something I had never come across before but was reliably informed were animal's testicles.

(I'm still trying to work out if putting one of those in your mouth is even legal.) Tenth, and just to finish off, half a dozen slices of toasted, doorstep thick granary bread, knee deep in butter, with lashings of Marmite, marmalade, strawberry jam or honey. (I did have a choice and wasn't forced to eat them all.)

Mark scoffed the lot at a single sitting, standing up, farting and belching simultaneously and in perfect pitch, then rubbed his belly saying, "I was ready for that!" I'm afraid I only picked at my breakfast, not doing it real justice: a bit of sausage here, a black pudding there, and a bit of fried bread to dip in my egg. I think the sweetbreads had put me off. I apologised to Mark for my poor showing, blaming it on the flat beer from the night before. No problem, Mark was still peckish and soon consumed everything that was left on my plate. Talk about eat for England: he could eat for the entire human race!

That evening we fished the night tide at Dungeness, a very famous venue for cod fishermen and one I had only read about before in angling

Mark and I have since gone on to enjoy numerous carp sessions together, and have enjoyed our fair share of success.

magazines. Mark led us to the hot-spot, directly behind the already-obsolete nuclear power station! As I recall it was by the outfall. As darkness closed in and the rising tide crashed up onto the shale beach a really eerie atmosphere set in: well at least to me it was; Mark and the other locals seemed immune to it.

It was like no venue that I had ever fished before. By the glow of the Tilley lamps you could see the kelp and seaweed showing up fluorescent in the waves! Actually it looked quite attractive: a whole area of about 500 square yards was glowing – positively radiating – in the dark. I sat on the shale looking up at my illuminated rod tip, expecting a spaceship to land at any second. It was like fishing in an amusement arcade.

Suddenly there was a 'donk, donk,' on my rod tip, and the rod, bent hard into my 6oz gripped lead, sprang straight. Up I leapt, striking in one movement, and ran back up the beach, winding down hard in the process. Then I felt the old familiar definite tug on the end of my line and knew that I had my first Dungeness fish. One hundred yards out I could see it glowing, fighting beneath the waves. Minutes later we were looking down at a small cod of four to five pounds. We didn't need the Tilley lamp: the fish out-illuminated the lamp by a good sixty watts!

Mark Lawson certainly knew his onions when it came to serving up breakfast, beach casting, and catching radio-active cod!

Mark said that he would fillet it straightaway so there would be no extra weight to carry back to the car.

"Are you sure about this mate?" I asked him. "Are you sure it is safe to eat?"

"Look mate, if you are worried there's an easy test we can carry out." He leant over, delving through his tackle bag. Eventually he climbed out, holding in his hand a light bulb. I look puzzled but Mark explained the procedure.

"Right then," said Mark, "you take the bulb and push it into the cod's mouth taking great care not to break it. Twist it slowly and try to get the terminals into the throat."

I looked on in amazement.

"Once you've done that and got it secure leave it twenty seconds and then whack the fish across the tail. This sends an electric charge up the spine."

Mark looked me straight in the eyes to make sure I understood this new technology.

"Yeah, yeah, je comprends monsieur," I bleated out, breaking into a sort-of French for some unknown reason!

"If the light bulb doesn't light up within twenty seconds then the fish is safe to eat," Mark continued.

"What if it lights up after twenty seconds? What then?" I naturally asked, having more faith in a Geiger counter than this new procedure for detecting radio activity. I was being educated, too.

"Well that depends," said Mark, "it all depends on how bright the bulb is. If it's just glowing, just all right, it's pretty safe to eat. If it's beaming like a lighthouse it could be dodgy. It's still edible, but not as tasty. You need lots of vinegar on it."

This bright young man who'd been writing to me for all those years obviously knew his onions!

The Big O, & Squatter Repellent

There are some things in life which it pays to steer clear of – politics, religion, controversy, and trying to understand women spring to mind: they all bring confrontation and life is hard enough without bringing any more pressure on yourself that you don't need. My life has been about walking that fine line between paying the bills and getting some quality fishing time, in between the football and still trying to be part of a family relationship.

I have a very simple philosophy when it comes to my fishing. If I am on a known big fish-water I set my plans out to catch the biggest; if I am on an unknown quantity, I fish for bites and try to catch every fish I can in order to get some idea of the potential of that water. I have been very fortunate, I think, in that fishing for four decades before the big carp boom, I was able to fish hundreds of waters, both in this country and throughout Europe, of unknown potential. Pioneering is as close to the edge as you can get in carp fishing. By logically evaluating that a certain water should contain big fish, and then proving it does, gives you an incredible buzz.

There are thousands of small lakes throughout Europe which, from time to time, get engulfed by the brute force of the Continent's massive rivers. What are in many cases already substantially-sized fish (fish which have grown large despite fighting currents, floods, droughts, barges and pollution) can literally become marooned in small, often weedy, angler-free gravel pits and pools which abound in all the major river flood plains. Already good-sized fish, transplanted by nature into small, rich waters, with no competition for food, can easily grow on to become fish of record-challenging proportions. So, my tip of the month is that any water, whatever the size, particularly when in a river flood plain, is well worth investigating. Every time a lake is flooded by a river everything changes, sometimes for the better, sometimes for the worse. While some waters may lose known good fish, as happened in the Colne Valley in the mid-80s, others acquire them. Every year unknown big fish get caught from small waters after floods die back, so don't just stay with the waters that are known, try those insignificant-looking waters, whatever the size, close to the rivers. Their life is an ever-changing landscape: you can never know what is in them after floods recede. This type of water can become exceedingly rich, with deposits of healthy, nutritious silt from the rivers every time they flood.

It was a chance meeting which reminded me of this tale. Like most chance meetings, it happened in a pub. One lunch-time I bumped into an old carp fishing adversary in a local pub – I use the word 'adversary'

Big fish can turn up unexpectedly in small lakes so all waters are worth investigating.

because in the 60s and 70s carp fishing was very secretive and, because of this, became very competitive. People were learning that certain techniques, allied to certain baits, would catch carp. The hard part in those days was finding waters with big fish in them. Big fish were, at that time, twenties; a 20lb carp would certainly win you a prize in the weeklies. Very few people had caught a twenty; a thirty was a dream, a dream which most anglers just didn't think about. The race was on to be first to get on potential big-fish waters; waters with potential were what everyone was seeking.

So, back to this bloke in the pub, who reminded me of a certain episode in my life and an insight into where my head was at that time. Why, thirty years on from our first meeting, I should now be talking to this man, I don't know! The first time I caught a glimpse of him I put it down to the sun in my eyes. I was baiting up at a local lake. I had a doddle of a job at the time and was in charge of the work's van. I would pick up the Grimsby lads at six in the morning and get them to work at Cottam for 8.00 a.m. On the way back I would bait up three or four lakes I fancied with the magic maples. By the time I got to fish the lakes it truly was very easy: the fish would simply come in each day for their food. I don't think there is any greater edge than a prebaited swim on a virgin water – certainly not when we're talking about this early-70s period. If you had the enthusiasm and the time available to implement your plans, carp fishing could look very easy.

On this particular day I had popped into this lake and fired out a bucketful of the Maple Mix. Fish were showing everywhere. I then shot down to another tiny pool, only ten minutes away, and put in another bucketful.

The fish had been so active when I had baited the first pit I had to shoot back to see if the fish were on the bait. You could not envisage the sight I was presented with – the swim was an absolute cauldron of bubbles, it was just like a vast kettle boiling; it was as though every carp, every bottom-feeding fish, even the odd nuclear submarine, was in on the bait.

There was I, thinking I was going to absolutely murder them on opening night when, amongst the cauldron of bubbles, up pops a frogman! This is for real! On the opening night of the previous season, I had caught the largest fish in the lake. In the weeks leading up to the coming season this guy had been watching me with the binoculars from the top of a tree on the bank opposite, and when I wasn't there he investigated the swim with snorkel and flippers!

He emerged like a walrus with a pipe thrust down his throat. What could I say? He was a keenie and wanted to know what bait I was using. I suppose if he had asked me I would have lied, because that's how things were in those days.

Bait has always intrigued anglers, ever since the first one wet a line. I can't remember the first fishing book that I read, but it contained an account of Arthur Buckley's then-record carp from Mapperley. The bait that had caught that monster fish was bread paste flavoured with honey.

"Why did he do that?" I thought. "Is honey something fish can't resist?"

Bait was already something almost mystical. Reading of that capture, I thought, still being young, that the bait had been the sole reason for the fish being caught. I had yet to learn of the right time, the right place, indeed, the right water. However, I should have realised some of those aspects because at one time I kept fish in a zinc bath. As a kid I was crazy for everything to do with nature: I had birds in the shed, rabbits and guinea pigs in a van in the garden, and I bred mice in a box under my bed. It was a nice little earner, actually; I used to sell them at school for three pence each. My parents actually encouraged me with this – that was until the day I swapped six mice for what I was told was a grey hamster. Mother passed out when she found me feeding a huge rat on the kitchen table!

Anyway, back to my fish. During the summer holidays, a local farm pond had dried up, and in the mud were lots of fish weighing, I suppose, 4-6oz. I used to go along to the pond tadpoling and newting with the other kids from our street, so we always had nets and buckets or jam jars with us. On that occasion we went home with every vessel we could find crammed with fish – we didn't even know what kind of fish they were: even the older boys from our estate who went fishing every Sunday on the match bus were unable to identify them. In the early-50s carp, in Lincolnshire at least, were as rare as hen's teeth.

I kept my fish in the bath. It was made out of zinc and spent most of its life outside, next to the shed. Once it got cold in the autumn months it would be brought inside once a week when the family took a bath. Having a bath in the late-40s/early-50s was very much a pecking order thing. Dad would have the first one with two kettles of boiling water poured in. The hotter the water, the more the soap lathered up. The first night dad took a bath we had a fish kill; I think I lost four fish – I had forgotten to tell my parents that I had fish in the bath.

After that episode I would transfer the fish on the Friday evening to a large bucket. They hated it and never settled until they were back in the old bath. I have to admit it, I used to fish for them on the odd occasion (about twice a day!). I pretty soon learnt that the first hour and the last hour of the day were the best times to catch fish – in a zinc bath, that is. I cracked that bath but I never had a take out of the bucket, and I gave it my best shot!

Looking back on it now, and trying to put it all into perspective, I would feed those carp every night with scraps from the table, and there weren't an awful lot of those. I think food was still rationed and the birds, mice, guinea pigs and rabbits also had to be fed. My abiding memory of this time is (I had now found out that my fish were king carp) that when those fish were hungry they would eat almost anything. They didn't particularly like stewed rhubarb but, even then, if there was nothing else they would eventually eat it. In a tiny environment like a zinc bath, just being fed each day can be much more than a carp ever receives in a natural environment. Since those times, as I've kept fish in tanks and fed them each day with my own carp feed and within six months they have outgrown the tank. It was a bit like that with dad: he put on two stone throughout the summer months and all his friends started calling him Clarissa!

Back to the point of this. Even in tanks or baths, even with a constant oxygen supply, which is not the case in their natural environment, carp still display their natural behaviour. If a tank has no artificial light, carp feed best during the first two hours of light and in the hour before dark. If there is a constant light on they will feed regularly around the clock. It is small wonder really that illuminated areas, such as marinas on rivers and canals, are often the most productive areas. On still-waters also, this can be the case. Just off the top of my head I can think of three waters in this county, all-purpose waters, where boats are moored up, and those illuminated areas are again the best spots on the water; they can produce around the clock.

I get many letters from young anglers asking about whether light at night scares fish. My opinion is this: constant light certainly does not, that is, a light which remains in one spot throughout the night-time hours; it may even be beneficial. Dick Walker was the father of carp fishing and in his book, Walker's Pitch, is a photograph of a carp taking a floating crust in the beam of a cycle lamp! In the 50s and 60s, fishing a margin crust in the beam of a torch was an accepted, successful, carp fishing technique. However, lights flashing all over the place at night may well scare fish, although I have a feeling that they annoy other anglers to a far greater extent. When I am all settled in behind the rods at night, relaxed, feeling part of the water, part of the landscape, nothing infuriates me more than flashing lights coming down my bank. But maybe that is just me.

I grew up on margin fishing, and I am never happier than when I'm able to fish close-in: indeed, many of my best fish have come from the margins. When you are fishing close, you just know when the fish are there on your bait. I personally swear that, at times, I can feel their hearts beating. The closer to the fish, the greater the intensity of that special 'I'm carp fishing' feeling.

The Big O with one of the start-of-season big fish he caught on my bait.

**Fishing with Ritchie in the early Eighties. "He's the Big 'O',"
said Ritchie, "Out of Order my son."**

Well, back to the story about the bloke I met in the pub, the bugger who, thirty years previously had snorkelled my swim to find my bait! Come to think of it, that story itself needs an end. It is basically this. He found my secret wonder bait, i.e. maple peas, and on opening night of that season – which for once I couldn't make as I was enjoying a successful Redmire rota session with Chris Yates – he fished my baited swim and caught the two largest fish in the lake! I think it understandable that I didn't speak to the bloke again for another twelve years – not that our paths crossed much during that period, which was probably best really, because for a time I had the right hump with him.

Years later I related that story to Ritchie Mac.

"That geezer's got some front," said Ritchie. "He's the Big O."

"What's the Big O, Ritch?" I asked.

"He's out of order, my son, out of order."

So there we were, Big O and me, elbows on the bar, glasses in hand, barely making conversation, when in walked a mutual farmer friend of ours. We gave it the usual:

"All right mate, how's things going?"

He was not talkative and clearly under strain. However, a couple of pints later he slowly started to bare his soul. During the summer our area had seen quite a bit of musical activity. Some quite decent travelling bands, representing all kinds of music, had been gigging at local village halls, and pubs were putting on groups on a regular basis. We even had a 48-hour rave in a local field. Music fans had been drawn from all over the country and some of them decided that they liked it so much that they set up camp on our friend's land; he had his own little hippy community down the bottom of his track!

Now our friend had nothing against them, in fact, he had talked to a few and said that they were jolly nice people, but they were in the way. He couldn't get through to his fields: he was worried about the wildlife on the site, and he was worried about litter. He was just finishing recounting his fears when in jumped Big O with:

"No problem, he'll get rid of them for you." Pointing at me, he carried on, "He can get rid of anybody."

I was astounded: I sounded like a hit man, and I didn't have a clue what he was talking about. I wasn't happy with it at all. I like to keep my head down.

"You remember," he said to me, "Squatter Repellent."

I vaguely remembered it. It was that bait thing again. Bait evolves: you start at one place and end up at another. I have written about it since the 60s, but it was always about the successful baits which were user-friendly, wife-friendly, socially-friendly. Squatter Repellent was one which fell by the wayside: even crows and magpies turned up their beaks to it. Every bad, insulting word that you can think of applied to that bait; 'odious, obnoxious, and disgusting' are complimentary when applied to it. It's a long story.

When I came out of the Redmire syndicate in the mid-70s, I thought I had the world at my feet. I had five or six great baits which I was sure would catch carp from anywhere carp lived. I felt I truly knew what particle bait to use for each occasion. I don't want to sound big-time, but everywhere I fished, I caught. This was at a time when carp were not thick on the ground and we would literally go to the opposite end of the country just to fish in the knowledge that a water contained carp. I once called Redmire 'The Aquarium' because it was a water where, from the top of a tree, you could literally see what carp did, how they behaved, how they fed. After imagining for years what carp did, at Redmire you could observe it, and see what actually happened. I learnt more about carp in three seasons there than I had learnt in the previous ten. It was a wonderful education.

So, let loose on the carp waters of the southern counties, which were actually very under-fished in those days, life was rosy: life was good, and most times you could catch fish. Even if you didn't catch a carp, you would get monster tench, bream, roach, or eels. I had, during my early fishing years, fished specifically for those species but the fact of the matter is that my personal best of all those species, roach apart, came whilst fishing for carp. Even my best pike came jagging a boilie in front of its head on the last day of the season when I found it tight under the bank by the old Snag Tree on the Canal Bank. All these captures came whilst trying out new, relatively young, gravel pits.

Particles were my thing until, that was, one day on Larkfield I was introduced to Fred Wilton. I got to know Fred well during the couple of years I was fishing Johnson's and its surrounding waters. Fred's theories and the results on his baits left my head in a spin: I was bouncing off the wall. In no time I was trying to formulate my own HNV baits based on fishmeals, supplemented with oils. By the time I had graduated to the Savay syndicate I had come up with my own Seafood Blend and the results were very impressive. Then, one day, I had a brainwave. Thinking back to my early working life on the Grimsby docks, I remembered a natural product which just had to be the dog's doodas. It was highly nutritious and full of oil, namely, dogfish livers.

Prior to my next trip to Savay I went down to the docks and bought two stone (28lb) of the said wonder bait. It was supplied in two muslin bags. I had not got halfway through my journey when the smell had become unbearable. I swear I drove the last 60 miles with my head out of the window of the old Renault 4. It was a stinking hot day and by the time I turned into the car park the dogfish livers had disappeared. They had actually melted and had run into every nook and cranny of the vehicle. The smell was something else. It was so bad that when, at the end of my trip, the car wouldn't start, and I had to call a mechanic to attend to it, he refused! There really is no smell like it.

A couple of years later, I bumped into the Big O on another local water. I had cooled down by now and had forgiven him for our first encounter. He was having big problems. He had a small cottage and whilst away working, squatters had moved into it. The council could not help him, the police could not move them on, and he was desperate. I said that I knew of something, and recounted the tale of the dogfish livers.

The following night, under cover of darkness, Big O poured a couple of litres of melted livers through the letterbox. By dawn, the squatters had fled, and Squatter Repellent was born. The cottage was uninhabited for a couple of months whilst he had the floorboards torn out and replaced, but that obnoxious mixture had done the trick.

Glimpses of the Past

I have never dreamed of catching a record carp, not even a local one, let alone a national or international record fish. I have never wanted to catch X amount of carp in a session, or a season. I can truthfully say that I have never tried to catch more fish, or larger carp than any other angler you might name, and I could never, ever, devote large amounts of time to the pursuit of a single fish.

If I have had any goals or ambitions on the fishing front they have been simply to do as well as I can with my allotted time. Increasing the size of one's personal best I do find very satisfactory, which I think is only natural, but I do not go out fishing every year with that intention. Fishing to me has to be an enjoyable experience. I could never grind it out on a water I did not like just to improve my personal best figures, nor could I handle looking over my shoulder all the time wondering if I was going to get nicked for night fishing. Add to this the fact that I cannot stand crowds and you will begin to realise why I'm rarely seen on the circuit waters. My carp fishing began in an era of peace, solitude and unspoilt waters and it was those aspects as much as the fish which I was attracted to.

Today I feel no different and I still search for waters offering that peace. If on occasions I find such a place which also has big carp then I'm a happy man. The greatest thrill I have experienced in carp fishing is tackling the unknown: lakes where the potential is all in the mind and not on the grapevine: where carp don't have names and success, as it should be, can only be judged on your own results. Finding such a place is becoming harder with each passing day, but still we try. The eternal chase for the end of the rainbow and the pot of gold!

We all want different things from our carp fishing, which in many ways creates different cliques and attitudes. Yet we are all bound together by the common love of carp fishing. To each his own: as long as you enjoy being there it's enough in my book. It may be hard for carp fishers of today to believe but in the early Sixties, although our enthusiasm was immense, we caught very few carp at all. Indeed, to catch a carp of any description was worth informing the then-small angling press about. Catching a carp was a true event and as such the capture tasted so much sweeter than a capture which is commonplace, as is often the case today.

Of course we knew very little about carp. When I think back to 1961 when I started out after this then-mystical quarry – never dreaming that I would still be after them all these years later – I guess that the sum total of my knowledge of the species was that carp had fins, swam in water, and that a famous angler by the name of Dick Walker once caught a big one on a piece of bread. Armed with such knowledge how could we fail? Quite easily, I can assure you!

I never meant to get involved with carp, never felt an obsession: it just kind of grew without me being aware that it was doing so. I'm sure the true addiction was simply a love of the outdoors. There was wonderment about being around a lake at night and watching and hearing the secrets of nature unfold. Then fishing night sessions was, in truth, quite scary. Each strange sound, each movement of the rushes, each rustle of the leaves would send a chill down the spine. There was no sleeping on the rods in those days: you were too scared to! Yet those were precious nights and days living experiences few fellow humans would ever know: watching animals and birds perform rituals others could only read about in books.

It was during those early times that I used to fish a small, tree-lined pool in my home county of Lincolnshire, often in the company of a friend from our football team called Derek. The sessions usually only lasted for one night, that night being Friday, the rest of the weekend being taken up by football commitments. We would sit side-by-side fishing into a small bay where carp occasionally betrayed their presence by throwing up huge masses of bubbles. In hindsight our earliest tackle was totally inadequate consisting of split-cane match rods and line around the five pound strain. We usually free-lined, using all manner of baits from bread and cheese to maggots and hemp.

Our usual tactic was to put a lead on the hook, cast it onto the opposite bank, which was only about twenty five yards away, and then walk round, bait the hook, lower it carefully into the margin, then spread maggots or hemp around it. Occasionally we had runs but almost invariably we would lose them due to the hooklink breaking. Looking back it is quite clear to me that we were, in fact, bitten-off and that our freeline tactics never gave us sufficient indication to minimise the risk.

I never felt it was an obsession: the true addiction was simply a love of the outdoors and tree-lined pools.

But it didn't really matter if we caught a carp or not: each session was a real adventure. Most nights we would fish under brollies but for good measure, if it looked as though heavy rain might well be encountered, we draped an old canvas sheet acquired from a wrecked lorry over the lowest branch of a stout tree just behind where we fished. This improvised tent practically became home once the north winds started blowing during early autumn.

One Friday night in late September I'd been away out of the area working and I arranged for Derek to take my tackle down to the pool: I hoped that I would be able to join him somewhere around seven in the evening. As it was the job took much longer than anticipated and it was well after ten when our foreman from work dropped me off on the road adjacent to the pool. It was pitch black and I had great difficulty finding my way along the winding track that went through the trees and down to the pool. We were very keen then and despite the difficulty I was having I never dreamt of switching on a torch or shouting to Derek for directions in case I scared the fish. A heavy footfall, or one moment of madness could have wrecked a week's preparation!

It really did seem to take forever but somehow I made it down the path in the direction of my friend. I couldn't see him but knew I was near; his snores were prevailing even above the sound of the wind through the trees. I don't know why I did it – let's just call it the mischievousness of youth – but I couldn't resist such an opportunity. Derek had always been a bit of a wind-up merchant and a few times I had been the victim of his practical jokes. Now was the time to pay him back.

He was beneath the draped canvas and with it being in a position directly between us there was no possibility of him seeing me, even when he awoke. First of all I grabbed hold of a branch of a tree that extended to behind where Derek was sleeping and began gently twitching it, rustling the leaves in the process. Derek wasn't impressed: he snored on. Not deterred I searched the ground at my feet in the darkness for some type of missile. I was in luck. The old tree beneath which he was sheltering was an oak and the ground was liberally scattered with acorns. Having collected about a dozen acorns I started gently lobbing them in the air so that they landed with an audible 'thud' on the canvas. Derek never stirred, and his snores seemed to get even louder!

I couldn't believe it: Rip Van Winkle had nothing on this guy. So, putting my hand around the side of the canvas I threw a handful of acorns in the direction of his snores.

"Arr, woo! What the hell? Who's there?" he yelled as he leapt in the air. It sounded like I'd scored a direct hit.

Having woken him now the real fun could begin! Derek began prodding things, shaking the rushes in front of him with his landing net and indulging in all sorts of other measures to scare off anything in the area. All the time I kept still, biting my lip to stop myself from laughing. After ten minutes of chain-smoking it sounded as though he had calmed down and I heard his bedchair creak as he lay back down. I just gave him time to settle down before I ran my finger-nails down the canvas. The bedchair creaked again as I startled him. Then, scratching quite furiously, I let out a ghostly tormented cry!

Derek snapped, leapt off the bedchair and started knocking the hell out of the canvas with a rod rest, muttering all sorts of obscenities in the process. I couldn't stand it any longer and just fell on the ground, consumed with laughter.

"You bathtub; you flippin' bathtub!" or words to that effect he yelled at me in a furious temper. He barely spoke to me for the rest of that session but by Sunday lunch time with a football match behind us we were drinking in the pub and all seemed forgotten.

Or was it?

A fortnight later for some reason Derek couldn't make our Friday night trip to the pool so I went on my own. By that time of year the nights were getting quite cold from the outset so I set up camp beneath the old canvas. There was quite a lot of activity that night with a couple of tench being quickly landed followed by several fish rolling over the baited area. By the sounds they made and the large ripples that lapped my bank I was in no doubt that the carp were active and were on the bait. It was just a question of time before I struck into one of the big fellows.

All evening long the lines twitched with line bites, until shortly before ten when the silver foil indicator glided confidently towards the butt ring. Putting in the pick-up I waited for the line to tighten then struck firmly over my right shoulder. The rod immediately doubled over and the unseen fish tore off to my left out of the bay with a power I had never before experienced. The old Mitchell clutch screamed out for several seconds then – nothing. The rod flipped back to the upright and the line flapped in the breeze. I was totally gutted.

I fell back onto the bedchair, shaking like a leaf. I tried to roll a cigarette but my hands were trembling so much it proved impossible. That night should have been *the* night, but I sensed that it was not to be and that my chance had gone. I cursed loudly to myself, as much in annoyance as disappointment.

I was not a happy man. I sat there, steam coming out of my ears, when there was a strange asthmatic kind of snort from the other side of the canvas. I sat upright, alert, not sure what it was. Listening intently I made out a heavy breathing, which was interrupted by another of those strange snorting sounds. I'd heard nothing like it before. It was strange, and very eerie. Then the scratching began; slowly at first, but building up to a furious pace. As it got louder and louder objects started hitting the canvas. Then the penny dropped! It had to be Derek getting his own back on me! But as he didn't know I knew what he was up to I decided to fix him for sure this time.

The snorting and heavy breathing had intensified and was now going on literally against the base of the canvas. Getting down on my knees I silently bent towards the canvas. I put my hand under it then quickly lifted it, at the same time letting out a blood-curdling scream and shining my torch straight into my protagonist's face.

For a moment my eyes wouldn't focus because of the sudden light but when they did I was in for a real shock. I found myself face to face all right, not with Derek but a badger! Momentarily we both froze! Then I involuntarily screamed, leapt back and smashed my head against the oak tree. The badger behaved in a similar fashion. It screamed, leapt backwards, and fell in!

There was an almighty commotion in the margin before it pulled itself onto the bank, then trundled off into the darkness. Now ordinarily I like badgers but I can assure you that the sight of those huge canine teeth a foot from your face in the middle of the night is not the most pleasant experience. In fact it scared the life out of me! I didn't sleep a wink that night, and never had another bite.

As I learnt more about catching carp in the following years I went on to catch some very nice carp from Pinetrees, but my everlasting memory of the pool is of the night I had my encounter with the badger.

On what now seems like a thousand nights or more Annie and I made our way on unsteady legs down the pot-holed track to the Mere in France. For every step forwards we tottered three steps back. The farmer's calvados was renowned for taking no prisoners and we were well and truly under the influence.

Contrary to rumours it was not our custom to get drunk at night. Our fishing time was, unfortunately, severely limited due to work. We were lucky if we could get away for four weeks each year, and weren't privileged enough to have the thirteen-weeks-a-year perk of the teaching profession, which a number of anglers enjoy. We had to make the most of our chances and make it happen and that meant being on the rods, in a fit state, during the productive periods. That was always our aim but sometimes, as on this occasion, we could get side-tracked.

We had been on the Mere for two days without a take. I wasn't too surprised as I'd got to know the water quite well. It fishes best during

The farmer's mere where we enjoyed numerous happy sessions.

the summer months when there is a good blow on it. When, as had been the case during our first two days, there is not a breath of wind you are going to struggle. The upside of this, if there is one, is that with few nuisance species present, by the time the weather does change a big bed of bait has built up: past experience had shown that in these circumstances a change in conditions could lead to some real bumper catches. After two days of nothing we were anticipating such action and not being on our rods was the last thing on our minds. But, as I said earlier, sometimes you get side-tracked!

The previous year we had made friends with Roland, the farmer whose land skirts the Mere. Roland and his sons were soccer fans of the old school; admirers of what Pele called "the beautiful game". As with

We had to go and play football just when the lake was about to kick off! When we came back the fish were there, and feeding.

We had spent two days waiting for the conditions to change and the fish to start feeding, and eventually they got their heads down big style.

me, while a win was important for our team, of more importance was the way the team played, and that meant with style. We were all fans of Glenn Hoddle, then playing in the French league for Monaco, and whenever they were on the television Roland would invite us round to watch the game. So any day Roland came round to say, "Wednesday, football," I presumed it meant Monaco and Hoddle were on the box. However I couldn't understand why Roland and his sons had taken to jogging round the lake in the evening: they were not what you would call your average fitness fanatics!

Well at 6.00 p.m. on the third day we were anticipating a run at any moment. A south westerly had sprung up which seemed to be growing in force by the minute. Conditions looked perfect. Then Roland approached the bivvy saying:

"Rod, one hour; the big game."

Oh no, that was the last thing I wanted! I tried to explain that the conditions were good and that on this occasion I would give the telly a miss, only to be told that I wasn't going to watch, I was going to play! It was the night of the big annual match between the local village and another rival village some ten kilometres away.

I must have laid it on a bit thick when I'd told Roland of my footballing youth! He had told the village that he had a former international (me!) turning out for them! Revenge would be sweet after the village had suffered a massacre the previous year. I'd really done it this time, and there seemed to be no way I could avoid it. I thought the best way out would be to feign injury after half an hour – that was if the old legs would last that long! Not having played for five years, and having put on a couple of stone in that time, it was doubtful if I could last thirty minutes. A new plan was hastily drawn up. The fish were surely due on the baited area at any time. We didn't want them eating all the bait out there before we got back to the swim, then departing. So I quickly rowed out in the boat and spread a five-kilo bucket of maize on top of the bed of boilies already out there. Back to the swim and new hookbaits were quickly rigged up and secured in the butt rings. Everything was set so we could

nnie with a typically
rgeous Mere mirror

get the baits back out within minutes of getting back.

The big match was something else! Before it started Roland introduced me to everyone as "Mon ami Rod, international." Talk about pressure; you'd have thought I'd signed on for Milan!

The rules were not quite the same as those that I was accustomed to. Each team consisted of about twenty players and the first half lasted as long as anyone remained standing. This happened to take about ninety minutes, the duration of a whole normal match! During the course of it someone would limp off and someone else would run on to make up the numbers. One of these substitutes was Annie, who played a blinder. Clearly not tutored in the art of football she ran around clattering any of the opposition who had the ball at the time, or who had recently had the ball, or who looked as though they might receive the ball! At times I shuddered at some of her tackles, and I was glad she was on our side. Me? I had a stinker. I should have scored at least half-a-dozen times having got myself into the right position, but I just couldn't put the ball away. If we'd played on till the following morning and their goalkeeper had gone home I'd still not have scored.

By the time it was all over we could hardly move. It felt like my legs had been encased in lead. Couple that with an abundance of alcoholic refreshments after the match and you can begin to understand why we ended up swaying on rubber legs at two in the morning!

By now the wind had dropped and the night air was completely still. There was almost complete silence, save for the occasional frog croaking in the reeds. With no signs of fish activity I couldn't help but think that we'd missed our chance; that the carp had been in, eaten all the bait and departed. But you never know, and without making the effort we wouldn't find out. So with legs well apart trying to maintain some sort of balance, out went the baits, cast in the direction of tree-top landmarks silhouetted against the night sky. On with the indicators and it was time to crash. The match had taken its toll: the wine had taken its toll: the calvados had robbed me of any energy I might have had left.

We slept through the dawn, and slept on through the early morning

42lb+. The biggest of the haul of nine fish in just over two hours.

sun. In fact we slept on until around 10.30 a.m. when I was suddenly into a screamer. What a relief it was as I finally laid a long, lean 34lb mirror on the unhooking mat. My head hurt like hell, and my body screamed out in pain. Quickly photographed the fish was away and I fell back into bed. My eyes didn't even have time to close before Annie was into another screamer, and soon another thirty was smiling for the camera. As much as we needed it we didn't get any sleep that morning. In the following two hours eight more carp were landed, the smallest weighing in at 29lb, the biggest going just over forty.

By today's standards, following the heavy fishing of lakes in the east of France, that catch might no longer be considered exceptional, but to this day it was the fastest, most concentrated sequence of quality fishing we have yet to encounter. Of course luck came into it, but to a certain extent you make your own luck. We love our carp fishing, but there have to be other things in life as well. I think it was the fact that on this occasion we had also experienced some of the other aspects of life that made the catch taste so much sweeter.

My only regret was failing to score a single goal the previous evening!

Mally – First Trip

Never, ever will I forget my first trip fishing together with Mally Roberts. I had met Mally on several occasions in the past but he could only recall the previous two. I had first met him at a specimen group meeting in the early Sixties. At the time he was fishing with another Hully Gullie angler who went on to become a very successful angler in his own right, and later a high-profile publisher. I can remember it like it was yesterday, although Mally hasn't the vaguest recollection of the occasion. He thinks he must have been in a previous incarnation at the time. The angler who was with him at that first meeting, Kevin Clifford, and I often try to jog his memory and although the light sometimes comes on there is never anyone there.

Even before that I knew that I'd met him in the early Sixties when I was playing in the band and Mally was something of a rock promoter. I have to admit that he never spoke to me much: I think he was jealous because my hair was longer than his! Anyway he booked us for four Thursdays running at the Gondola Club in Hull. I'm sure it was Mally with his pink spangled shell suit, long straggly platinum blond hair, medallions around his neck, and fingers all covered in rings. That was surely Mally, wasn't it?

He put together a Thursday night R&B and Blues Extravaganza. As we carried all the amps and instruments through the door, all huffing and puffing, we failed to spot the billboards hung on the walls of the venue:

That was us! Underneath was the following spiel.

THIS LEGENDARY BAND HAS PLAYED WITH ALL THE R&B, BLUES AND ROCK AND ROLL GIANTS, INCLUDING THE BEATLES, LITTLE RICHARD, FATS DOMINO AND PETERS AND LEE. THIS IS THEIR DEBUT IN THE UK AND NOT TO BE MISSED.

Rod the Mod from Grimsby (not Germany) in the days of The Pack

To be fair we had a great time until a handful of young ladies asked us for our autographs.

"No problem," I said to the first young lady, actually feeling quite proud. I think it was the first time I'd had this request.

"Oh, you speak such good English," she said.

I thought, "Well I would do, with you coming from Hull," not knowing that she thought I was German.

"Have you studied at an English university?" she asked, seeking enlightenment.

"No," I replied truthfully, having no idea what was coming.

"Then how come you speak such good English?" she asked.

"Because I come from Grimsby, love, it is what we speak on the

Mally and yours truly still in musical mode 40 years on and dressed up as the Blues Brothers for a fancy-dress occasion. We have the same tastes in music – and parrots.

other side of the river."

At that point a poster was rolled out in front of us revealing that we were Germany's number one band. After our first set of the evening we went off to rapturous applause. After our second set, when the audience had found out that we were from Grimsby, we were booed off the stage. No wonder I didn't see Mally for several years: I think my brother Dave was probably chasing him for our money.

Alice, Mally's mum, did not realise that there was any history between me and her son. All she knew was that a bloke from Grimsby – who Mally had apparently only met a couple of years before – had ferned (sorry, phoned) a couple of weeks earlier asking him if he fancied a month on an inland sea. Mally was enthusiastic and had gone for it, no questions asked. But Alice was protective of her boy and asked me to have a cup of tea with her while Mally loaded his collection of Morrison's bags into the back of my van. Alice wanted to tell me about the ups and downs of her son's life. I knew bits and pieces, most of it from back in my youth, but there was a glaring gap of about 25 years before I'd bumped into him again a couple of years previously. Alice wanted me to look after him. Now responsibility doesn't sit easily on my shoulders but Alice was speaking from the heart. I had always preferred to be the daft lad in class, and never ever aspired to be head boy. As I listened to Alice's story I knew it was finally time: I had to take up the responsibility baton.

I knew much of the past from the early years and Alice filled me in on the intervening period. There had been women, booze and drugs. He'd been addicted to Grecian 2000. His eyes weren't that good and he'd been unable to read the label. He'd been drinking it for two years, not knowing that he was supposed to massage it into his scalp. It was a sorry story. The rest of his time he had squandered. After the dark days he had broken out, knocked everything on the head and become a fitness freak. He spent his time at the gym, practising martial arts, swimming five miles in his lunch hour, biking twenty miles after work and then finishing with a ten mile jog! Alice put her head in her hands, looking distressed.

"All that fitness, Rod, it can't be good for him. Please try and slow him down."

Now she had come to the right bloke there! I was renowned for being as laidback as a slug on slug pellets. But it was time to be off. I drank my tea and made for the door.

"Rod he can wait another five minutes. I just want you to understand the pressure he's been under this last year with his recent troubles."

My ears stuck up like a rabbit's. I knew of no recent troubles. I had to listen to this hot new gossip straight from Alice.

The problem had started some three years before when Mally and all his mates who were looking after parks, paths, highways etc. had been given notice by the council and contractors brought in to do their jobs. Three years on it had become an all-too-familiar story to people nationwide. But our Mally during his time at the council had done all sorts of courses, and even degrees. His first step up the ladder of success had been changing the bulbs in the street lamps. Obviously having a head for heights he was soon head-hunted by the gardening department, his speciality being trees. He soon gained a reputation for his extensive knowledge. Even posh people away from the city with their country estates were requesting his advice, asking for him by name. (I wish they'd tell me what it was: I forgot it years ago, so I'll just stick to Mally.) All this posh totty used to walk Mally round their estates.

"Oh Mallikins, can you tell me what this gorgeous thing is?"

"It's a tree ma'am."

"Mallikins you're so precise, so decisive. Where do you get all of this knowledge, this utter confidence that what you are saying is correct?"

"I worked for the council, ma'am."

With all this respect Mally was commanding it was hardly surprising that he turned down a job offered by the new contractors at less money than he had been on before. He took redundancy and decided to have a go on his own as a gardening-come-tree consultant.

I was worried when Alice asked me to take responsibility for Mally on our trips. I gave up on responsibility early in my school days!

Listening to Alice everything seemed to have been going so right for her lad that I was beginning to wonder when his new problems arose. All was to be revealed.

With all his new qualifications Mally decided to target the posh end of the market, country estates and the like. To reach his intended audience he took out an advertisement in the prestigious Country Life magazine. Mall dictated the advert over the phone to some posh totty in the shires. It should have taken about ten minutes but with the language barrier it took over an hour. He had not even seen his advert when the orders came flooding in. The first job was at an old people's home. Nothing unusual there, thought Mally; they must have nice gardens and lots of trees to go at and he was assured there was plenty of work, with five jobs being urgent.

First day in his new job he got all spruced up, washing his wellies and even putting a tie on – over his scarf, I might add. He should have read his advert before he set off for the job, but he didn't. It had all been laid out beautifully, but there was a glaring mistake. Instead of reading 'Malcolm Roberts, qualified tree surgeon' it read 'qualified knee surgeon'! When his van pulled up outside the home and Mally jumped out with his chainsaw under his arm three patients went into cardiac arrest. He was threatened with writs, compensation claims, you name it.

"So you understand the pressure that he's been under. Look after him," said Alice. "Better get off now or you'll miss your ferry."

What a Man's Gotta Do...

Sometimes in life a man's gotta do what a man's gotta do, so you drink your milk, get on your horse, and do it... It had been getting to me, all those stories of those huge kippers from France. Stuck in the factory making bait, all the phone calls and letters were doing me no good at all; I wanted my share. What I wanted, what I craved for was a good session. Not just a few days rushing here and there in the hope of a fish, I wanted time, time to give one of the big-fish waters my best shot. By the time August had come around I'd made up my mind; I was going to have that session and hang the consequences. There was just one little problem to surmount, namely a driving licence. For reasons I won't go into I didn't happen to have one with me at the time!

**Loaded up and ready to go with Richard as my chauffeur and translator.
No rave tapes please!**

Now there are ways round everything and I was sure that a couple
of mates of mine would be up for it. Sure they were: the prospect of
sun, wine and big carp was a chance neither could turn down – until
four days before the planned trip when both unavoidably had to cry
off. Disappointed? I'll say I was. I could have topped myself. It was
reach for the revolver time again. Everything was going wrong and I
just couldn't believe it. I looked up towards the great carp man in the
sky and wondered what I'd done to offend him. Weeks had been spent
planning it all. The ferries had been booked, and all the bait had been
sorted out. I had a boat, engines, batteries, new line on the reels, rigs
had been tied up and the van MOT and insurance sorted out. I'd put
so much work into it that I was physically and mentally shattered. I
couldn't see all that hard work going down the drain. I was down in the
dumps and feeling sorry for myself when I thought, "What the hell, I
am going, let's make this thing happen."

Now I'm not the sort who can fish with just anyone. To me the fish are not everything. To really enjoy my fishing it has to be in the company of someone I can naturally get along with. Conversation can be very strained when the only subject you have in common is carp fishing: there have to be other topics of conversation or life gets very dull. I guess that's how friendships actually get made, because there is always something to talk about. But those I would have chosen to fish with either couldn't make it, or wouldn't. Where did I go from there? I was in desperate need of a chauffeur.

Richard Tennant, who worked for me then, could see I was starting to panic and suggested a friend of his, Richard Seal. Richard had just finished college, was in a position to go, and would probably jump at the chance. At first I declined the offer not believing that I could get on with someone half my age and knowing the stress and strains that can be part of any prolonged trip. Then it hit me: the trip was practically upon me. It had to be Richard or there would be no trip at all. Considering that I'd never met him it was a bit of a gamble, but one I felt it was worth taking. The only stipulation I made was that no rave tapes were allowed. I can handle most things in life but rave music isn't among them. It's like hitting yourself over the head with a hammer and I'm always glad when it stops.

Friday afternoon came round and the fateful day had arrived. Richard arrived, his brother Ben having driven him over the Pennines from Stockport. I recognised both lads, their pictures along with nice fish having graced previous issues of Carpscene. Soon we were into the monumental task of loading up the camper for a month's trip. This took several hours, involving the use of a fork lift truck to get everything up on the roof and out of the way. When at last it looked as though it had been completed Richard emerged from Ben's car with a box full of cassettes.

"I thought these would help the long drive," said Richard.

"Just as long as they're not that awful rave music," I replied.

Richard's face dropped and Ben started laughing.

"That's all he's got," said Ben.

Mud water and anglers as far as the eye could see.

I couldn't believe it. Obviously Richard Tennant hadn't passed my message on. Not the best of starts but surely things could only get better. Couldn't they? Well the ferry trip went well enough and the following morning we set off from Zeebrugge heading down through France. No actual destination had been planned but three waters were on my mind. For once I wanted to go for a really big fish, one that might improve my personal best. Two of the waters I had in mind had, in the past, produced such fish while my friends and I thought that the other had the potential to do so. To get to the last water involved travelling past the other two so the plan was to look at them all in turn and weigh up the chances. I should explain here that news of the first two had got out on the grapevine and there was a real possibility that there would be no space to fish on either water such was the pressure both had been receiving.

First port of call was the Orient. As luck would have it just as we were about to give up on the idea of fishing it because of the over-crowding in the very last area we checked some Dutch guys were just packing up. There still wasn't much room as there were German and French anglers in residence but there was just enough room to squeeze in at either end of them. We thought it was worth a shot.

After taking down just the minimum amount of tackle to secure his swim Richard returned to the camper for the night, knackered from the long day's drive. I decided to cast out a couple of baits with stringers, just a few yards out. Not that I was expecting anything but with a bait in the water you've always got a chance. As it happened I had runs all night long from tench (big ones) and carp (very small ones).

The following morning Richard appeared looking slightly worried.

"Rod, I've got the camper stuck and I can't reverse it out."

I looked back to see where he had parked it. No wonder he couldn't reverse out, he'd parked it on the equivalent of the North Face of the Eiger. To make matters worse it had rained all night and water was running down the steep slope like a river. Hitting him over the head with a bankstick I sent him off into the countryside in search of a farmer and a tractor. A couple of hours later he returned, complete with farmer, helper and tractor. Within no time the camper had been pulled out and was back on terra firma. We paid the farmer for his trouble then proceeded to unload the mountainous stack of tackle, bait and supplies.

By late afternoon, tired, sweating and half a stone lighter we were set up in our swims. Richard went off to park the camper in a safe place while I set about blowing up the inflatable dinghy. Half an hour later I was huffing and puffing and still hadn't got the thing up. It had been kept in a garden shed during the winter and the mice had taken a liking to it. I'd seen fewer holes in a string vest.

"All right?" asked Richard when he returned.

"No I'm not," I said, "mice have eaten my boat."

Richard was looking worried.

"What's up now?" I asked.

Richard stuttered a bit at first then came out with it.

"I've had a little accident. I just didn't see it there. I've backed into the German's car."

There was complete silence as I looked at Richard, hardly believing my ears and he looked at me wondering whether I was going to kill him or not! Before I could say anything Richard jumped in, trying to lessen the blow.

"I didn't do much damage," there was a pause, "well not to his car. The camper's a bit of a mess though."

"Should I kill him or get him to bait my swim first?" I wondered.

Funnily enough after that somewhat dodgy start for the most part things went fine. We had to put up with an inflatable dinghy that required patching each day, plus a rigid boat with only one rowlock and no seat. Great that was: you went round in circles while your knees either cramped up or you made yourself a candidate for Piles of the Year! Then there was the thick clinging mud and the endless procession of anglers enquiring as to when you'd be leaving, but generally we got on great and we caught a fair number of fish into the bargain. The following are some of the strongest recollections I have of the rest of the trip.

Dawn had only just come up and I was sitting outside the bivvy drinking and talking to a Dutch angler we had christened Robert the Rice Man. He was a nice bloke, easy to get on with, although our conversations never lasted very long due to the fact that he was a very frequent visitor to the bushes. His wife had prepared a meal for him for every day of the week, each of which was neatly wrapped and packed away in his cool box. The only problem was that each meal was exactly the same, rice, peas and a few prawns, hence the frequent visits, and hence the name Robert the Rice Man. Well we were chatting away when suddenly one of my rods absolutely rocketed off. I was straight into it and even at a range of about 350 metres the fish was taking line off the reel.

The social scene is one of the consolations when you are fishing the big, slow venues.

"I'll get my boat," said Robert, which seemed a good idea as mine was lying as flat as a doormat in the mud.

In no time at all we were ploughing through the water in pursuit of Mr. Cypry. Robert was a dab hand with the boat and soon we were above the fish, with me applying heavy pressure. I'd had a couple of small carp in the night and had got in a bit of a tangle in the dark so, not wanting to tackle up again, had put out the spare rod, my old Horizon, and this was the rod the run had come to. Now the Horizons have plenty of poke in them but this was a big fish and I just could not get it up into the surface layers. At one point I thought I had it beaten when suddenly there was a tremendous surge of power and down she went, nearly pulling me out of the boat in the process. I quickly banged the Baitrunner back in for fear the clutch wouldn't keep up with it and by the time I disengaged it all was solid. However this was one of the times when long leaders prove their worth and several turns were already on the reel.

"Go for it," said the Rice Man, so I heaved and heaved for all I was worth. Reluctantly something moved slowly up off the bottom. It felt just like a sack of cement. I kept on heaving, the old rod kept creaking, then let out a tortured cry and went 'crack'. The spigot had snapped. I was so determined not to let this one get away that I quickly grabbed the leader, pulled my sweater sleeve down and wrapped the line round it that so as not to sever my hand. I pulled and I heaved and I sweated and up she slowly came. Wrapping more line round my sleeve I heaved again, giving it all I'd got.

"She's coming Robert, get the net out," I yelled, all excited like you would be.

One last heave, Robert reached out with the net, and finally she broke surface. It was a roll of barbed wire fence.

"Do you think that took your boilie?" asked the Rice Man mischievously.

"Shut up," I said.

Now although I have picked up a little French over the years Richard was along not just as chauffeur but also as my official translator. He had studied French at school - and had even stayed on holidays with French families polishing his French language to a fine degree - and was enjoying the chance to engage in conversation in French again. He was chatting away to a farmer at the bar and the translated conversation went something like this:

"Nice weather we're having. Do you know if there is any wind or rain forecast?"

"Oh, I live in the next village," replied the farmer.

I burst out laughing.

The hard bit turned out to be one of my fillings, with somewhat painful consequences.

Richard with the biggest
fish of our five-week session.

"No, sorry mister, you misunderstood me," persisted Richard, "I asked if you know if the weather is about to change. Is any wind or rain forecast?"

"Oh, sorry," said the farmer in reply looking at his watch, "it's quarter to three."

Sunday night I was happily chomping away on my bankside speciality Cantonese fried steak, Lincolnshire style – washed down with an excellent vintage Côtes du Rhône – when I crunched on a hard bit. I gave it another bite to see if it was edible, then decided it wasn't. Examining the offending object I realised that it was not a tough piece of meat but a metallic filling which had dropped out of one of my ancient molars. With another week still to go and cold frosty nights ahead an empty cavity was a threatening proposition, and not one to look forward to. Being the practical fella that I am I sought a solution. The wine was doing its job and a flash of inspiration lit up the old grey matter: I put a drop of Superglue on the filling and popped it back into the tooth. Problem solved; job's a good 'un.

I thought nothing of it till the following afternoon, by which time my gum felt slightly sore. The night was quite hectic with a few runs occurring and it must have been close to four in the morning before I got any real shut-eye. By then the gum was extremely sore.

Next morning, waking at the crack of ten, I felt rough. It was one of those days when you know you're just not wired up right. Richard came round to see me with a cuppa and, on seeing me, stepped back in amazement and shock. Now I'm never a pretty sight in the morning, nor the afternoon, evening or night come to that, but on this particular morning I really looked like an old dog. One side of my face was literally twice the size of the other. Nick Faldo had obviously sliced a tee shot and the ball had become firmly wedged in my jaw. Richard was so concerned that he suggested we pack up straight away and head off back to England. No way: I was in too much pain to pack up and just wanted to lie there and die, besides which I had fish to photograph.

We caught plenty of carp but I
didn't get the big one I was after.

I forced myself through this ritual – all sideways on shots mind you because from the front I looked like a knobbly potato. Half an hour later I had to give in to the pain. I was in agony and my face was blowing up by the second, so off we went in search of a doctor.

Richard's French came in handy here. We visited a blacksmith, taxidermist and tattoo artist before we finally found a surgery and, with some trepidation, sat down in the doctor's waiting room. When we were eventually ushered into the surgery even the doctor looked shocked: he thought Richard had brought him the Elephant Man! Looking into my mouth he instantly picked up the phone and rang the nearest hospital. He sounded very concerned. I couldn't fully understand the conversation but the words 'enormous' and 'grotesque' were easily picked out. He didn't think much of the state of my mouth, either! He explained that although he could prescribe antibiotics the huge abscess which had formed needed lancing, but that he wasn't qualified to do it. So he'd made an appointment at the nearest hospital that afternoon.

We never kept that appointment though because shortly after we left the doctor's the offending lump in my jaw burst and went straight into my system. I felt rougher than rough, like I'd been drinking southern beer all night and had eaten a bad curry on top. The doctor's little pills did the trick though and after 20 hours or so sleeping it off I was ready for battle again.

Norfolk carp angler John Dunne once said to me:

"It's not enough to be a good angler, I'd rather be a lucky angler."

He was right of course, and over the years I've had more than my fair share of luck. But on this occasion luck had certainly run against me. I was now at the end of the long session and had just one night to go. Catching carp hadn't been a problem: I was averaging two or three a night but I just couldn't crack a really big one. This was my last chance. I was going to give it my best shot; a big 'un or bust. The rods were made up and the baits rowed out to the 350-metre mark. It wasn't proper fishing but sometimes a man's gotta do what a man's gotta do.

An hour after dark Richard and a couple of Dutch lads were sitting round my bivvy yarning and having a beer when the left -hand rod was away. I leapt out of the bivvy, kicking over everyone's beer, and was on it. The rod hooped over, then shot straight back

"Oh dear I've lost it; what a pity!" I remarked.

Everyone remained silent, sensing my disappointment. I presumed the hook had slipped out but on retrieving the tackle found that the fish had been feeding so confidently that the baited hook had been swallowed and I'd been bitten off.

"That must have been some fish to swallow that lot," said one of the Dutch guys, with which they returned to their rods thinking a few lunkers could be about.

Around midnight the middle rod was away. The outcome was the same in that I was again bitten off! I couldn't believe how my luck was running. The old proverb "Bad luck is better than no luck at all," came to mind, but I wasn't too sure about that one.

So there I was, tired, cold and disappointed, laid out on the bed trying to get some kip dressed in wet muddy chest waders, dreading the thought of packing up in the morning and facing reality, when at 3 a.m. the remaining rod burst into life. I was almost scared to pick it up fully expecting a bite-off again but no, my luck was in. Even at 350 metres it had me instantly back-winding. I wasn't going to lose this one. It was one of those heart-pounding jobs because I felt certain that this was my whacker. Wading twenty or thirty yards out into the water with waves crashing over me I played the fish as though my life depended on it. It felt so heavy I just couldn't get it up to the top, even in water only four feet deep.

The fight seemed to last forever when suddenly there was a big swirl in front of me. In the dark I just lifted the net and hoped for the best, then looked down into the net to admire my prize. There she lay in all her glory, the most perfectly conditioned five pounder I'd ever laid eyes on — all tangled up in someone else's tackle.

They say that bad luck is better than no luck, but I wasn't
so sure when I landed this little fella — all tangled up in
someone else's tackle. Oh well, back to reality...

I left the Orient behind with mixed feelings and a heavy heart.

That was the end of the adventure. After a five-week session packing up is a nightmare. Your session's gone and you're deflated. You've given it everything. You're talking about having to walk all your tackle 200 metres and more back to the motor through two feet of mud – and that's not just one trip but five or six. For a long session on the big French reservoirs you're not talking about the gear you need for a session in this country. You've got all the camping gear, the generator, the heavy batteries, the boat, the engine and so on. The list seems endless, and so does the packing up. It's an enormous task and with the days shortening at the end of October packing up and getting on the road can take all day. It's an absolute killer, mentally and physically, but it's part of the game and you take a deep breath and get on with it. It's part of the price of carp fishing and on this occasion the price was especially high because Annie and the kids would no longer be part of my life. I was going home to an empty house and facing the unwelcome prospect of picking up the pieces of my life yet again.

Shoot Out at Crazy Jane's

Back home from the Orient there was no family, no dogs, and, just to rub salt into the wounds, I'd been burgled as well. My music system was my pride and joy but it had flown the nest. I could never make light of this period, but somehow you get through it. I had my music back in and Sky Sports installed by the following night!

Slowly I started to get myself together and after realising that too much football can turn you into a couch potato I bought myself a mountain bike. I took it easy at first, limiting myself to trips to the nearest pub, a mile and a half away. After a week's practice I graduated to the next-nearest pub, two and a half miles away. I was gradually building up to The Wagon, which is two villages away.

I finally made it to The Wagon one night but some rotten sod pinched my lights! I didn't think it was safe to ride the main road home with no lights so I took the wild route along the old railway line. Even in the dark I knew it like the back of my hand: I'd walked my dogs down there dozens of times. Unfortunately no one had told me that the local farmer – shame on you John! – had put a barrier down across the line at night. I suppose that if I'd had lights I would have seen it, but instead I hit it face on. It nearly tore my head off! It hadn't been a good day. I'd had enough and rolled off into the path-side ditch to get my head down for the night.

The 'Wag' was a long ride even without the obstacle course and more and more I used to visit the pub a couple of miles away. I became a regular visitor to The White Horse, commonly known in the area as Crazy Jane's Saloon, and during the course of these visits became friendly with the barmaid Maureen Murphy. She was a fine voluptuous Irish lass who loved to have a laugh, although little did I know what she had in store for me. Jane's little pub was the best entertainment in the area: good food, music on all the time, pool table, lots of girls and live bands. I loved the place. There were some great characters I loved talking to, and all the time Murphy was quietly lining me up. I knew nothing about it but secretly Maureen had been match-making.

Two of my Dutch friends John Van Eck and Robert Paul were over for the weekend: just a few beers, watch the football, and then the boxing if we managed to stay awake – nothing heavy, just a nice easy social. So there we were, John and Robert and I having a beer when there was a lull in the conversation. Like a rat up a drainpipe in shot this obviously female voice. Sensing her moment of opportunity she yelled along the bar:

"You; I hate you!"

The three of us looked at each other wondering who she was pointing at. It soon became clear who the focal point of her admiration was: me! I tried the old Robert de Niro ploy to put her off.

"You talking to me? I don't see anyone else so you must be talking to me." Actually the pub was full and she could have been talking to anyone! "Did you say that you hated me?"

"Yes," came the firm reply.

"Look love you don't know me and I don't know you so how can you hate me?"

"Because you stink my house out," came back with real venom.

I tried a reasonable approach.

"Look there are a handful of nights in my life of which I have little or no recollection but as far as I know I have never visited your house. I don't even know where you live."

Secretly I was now having doubts. Surely some devilish fiend hadn't put one of my socks through her letter box?

It transpired that her son had the carp-fishing bug and was stinking her house out making bait. To make matters worse he was serious about it and was using Monster Crab. Now you really have to be serious to use this flavour. The closest you can get to describing its smell is to say it is like a cross between fermenting rotten crab, bad eggs and cat pee.

"It stinks," she carried on, "his clothes permanently smell of it. No wonder he can't keep a girlfriend."

And I thought it was just the way he walked.

As the night wore on and the white wine started to take effect she started to mellow. Actually I quite liked her. She was as daft as a brush and judging by her appearance had a hairstyle to match.

With the lads over for the weekend the night was already planned. A taxi picked us up at ten then it was a Chinese takeaway and back in time for 'Match of the Day', like blokes do. As we were leaving the lady asked me if I had been to see the seals yet. Every year grey seals invade our local beach where the females give birth amongst the sand dunes. Out on the water-line huge bulls chase the remaining females who haven't been serviced. How they know this I haven't a clue, but they do. This annual invasion of the beach was something I was well aware of, yet despite living in the area for over twenty years I had to admit that I was yet to witness it.

"I'll pick you up tomorrow and take you then," she said.

"O.K.," I said, "pick me up about three in the afternoon."

I knew that by that time John and Robert would have already left to catch their ferry. I had a growing feeling that I was going to be seeing quite a lot of the young lady. As I tried to get through the door of the pub she called after me:

"Oy, you haven't even asked my name. It's Coral, like in the ocean, you know?"

"Like in the bookies," I replied, disappearing into the night, and the future.

I had a growing feeling
I was going to be seeing quite
a lot more of the young lady.